Kindergarten Mazes

Simple Mazes for Kids

written by

Peter I. Kattan
and
Nicola I. Kattan

Petra Books

www.PetraBooks.com

Kindergarten Mazes: Simple Mazes for Kids.
by Peter I. Kattan and Nicola I. Kattan.

This is a book containing simple mazes for children in kindergarten - ages 4 - 8 years and up. All the mazes in the book are designed specially for these children in mind. There are 78 mazes in the book with seven levels of difficulty categorized as: Super Easy, Easy, Easy-Medium, Medium, Medium-Difficult, Difficult, and Super Difficult. The mazes increase gradually in difficulty from the beginning of the book till the end. This is a perfect book packed with learning and fun and will keep your kids entertained. Check our website at www.PetraBooks.com for more children puzzle books.

Kindergarten Mazes: Simple Mazes for Kids.
written by Peter I. Kattan and Nicola I. Kattan.

ISBN-13: 979-8-8691-9810-5

Kindergarten Mazes

Name: ______________________   Date: ______________

1. Super Easy

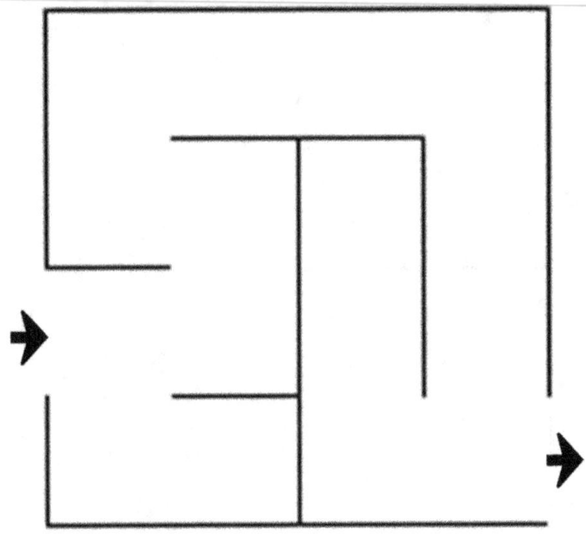

2. Super Easy

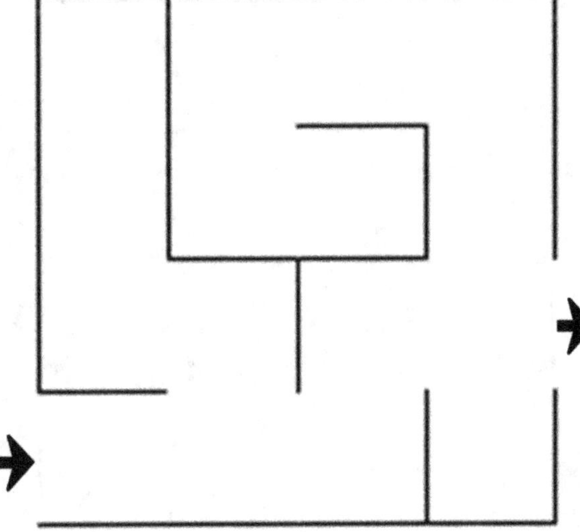

Name: _____________________ Date: ______________

3. Super Easy

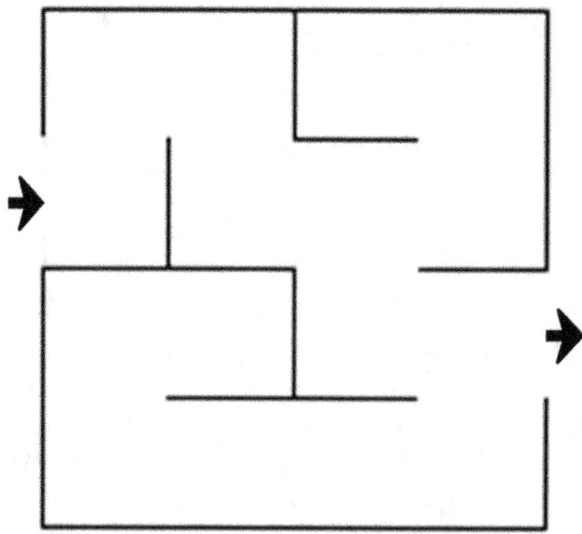

4. Super Easy

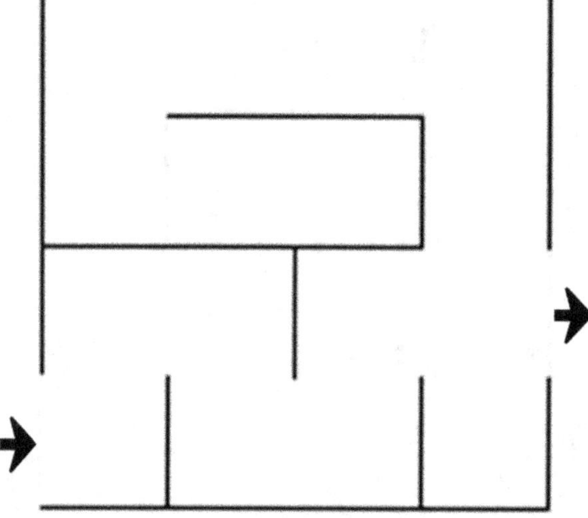

Kindergarten Mazes

Name: ___________________________   Date: _______________

5. Super Easy

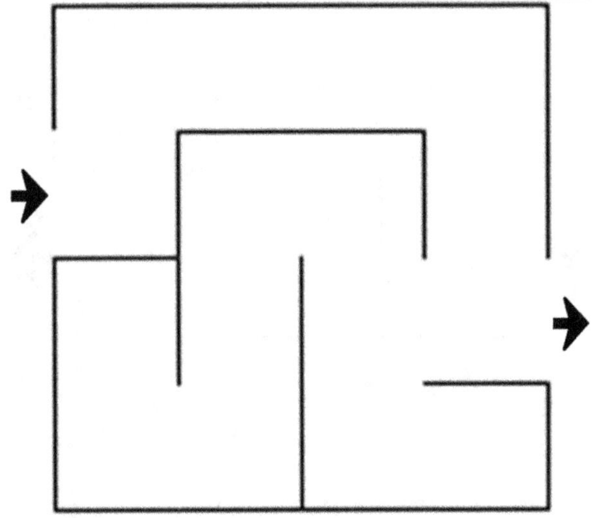

6. Super Easy

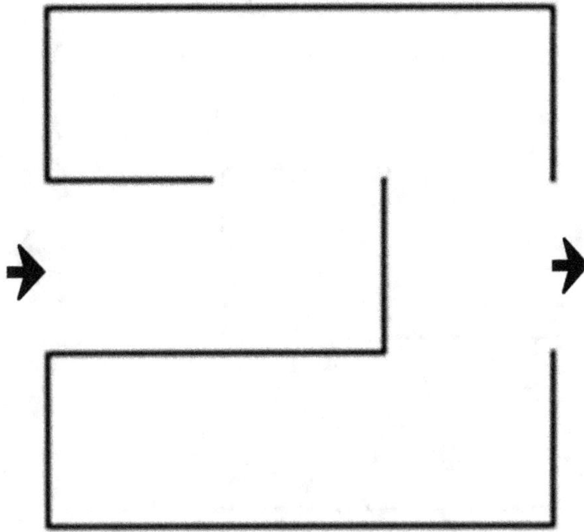

Name: _______________________   Date: _______________

7. Super Easy

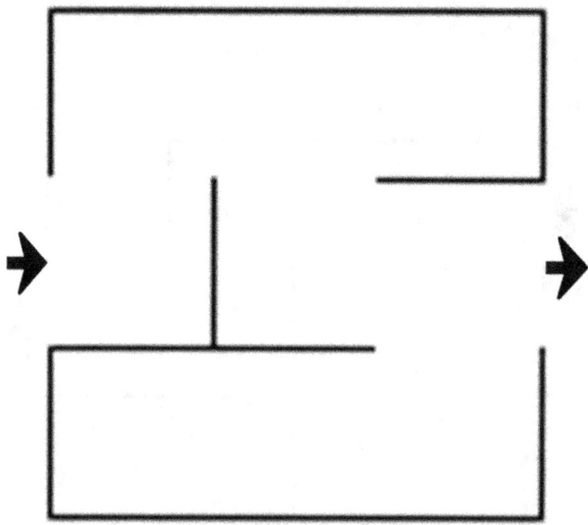

8. Super Easy

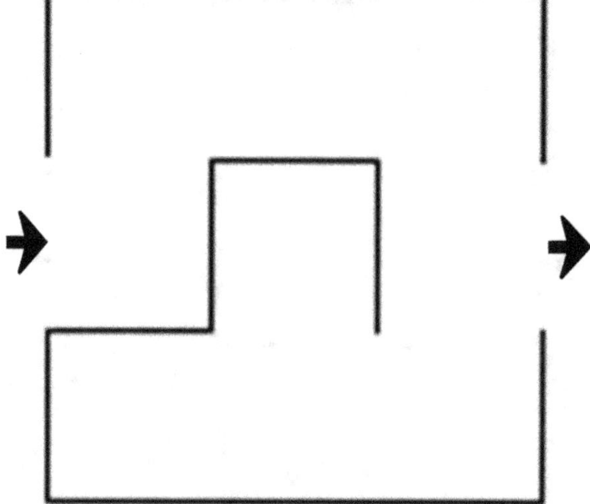

Name: ___________________   Date: ____________

9. Super Easy

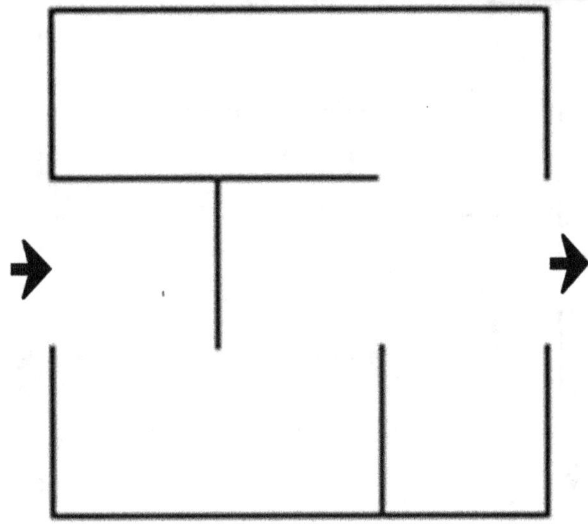

10. Super Easy

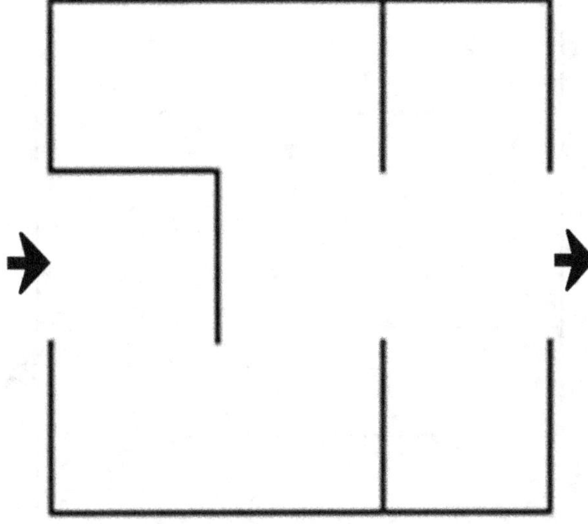

Name: _________________________   Date: _______________

11. Easy

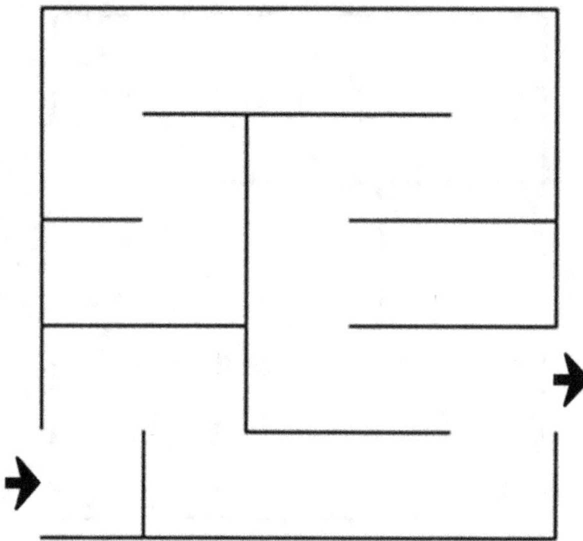

12. Easy

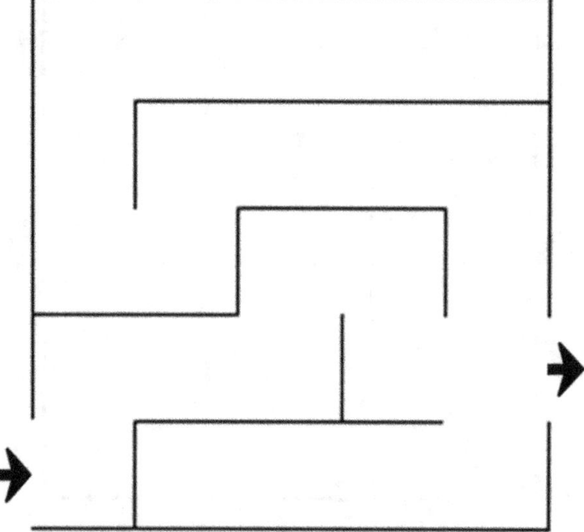

Kindergarten Mazes

Name: ___________________   Date: _____________

13. Easy

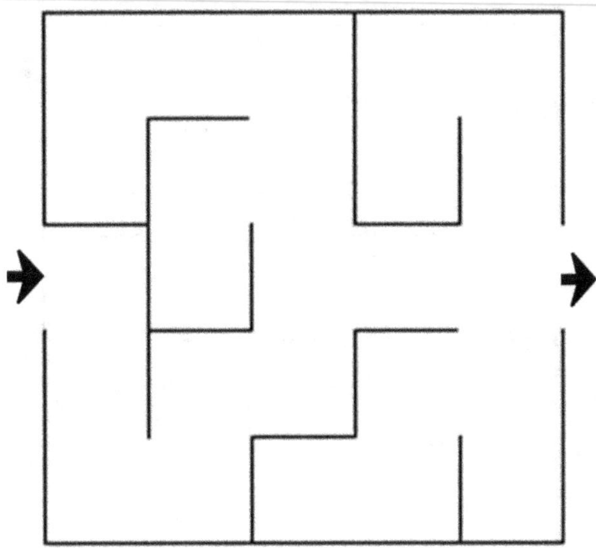

14. Easy

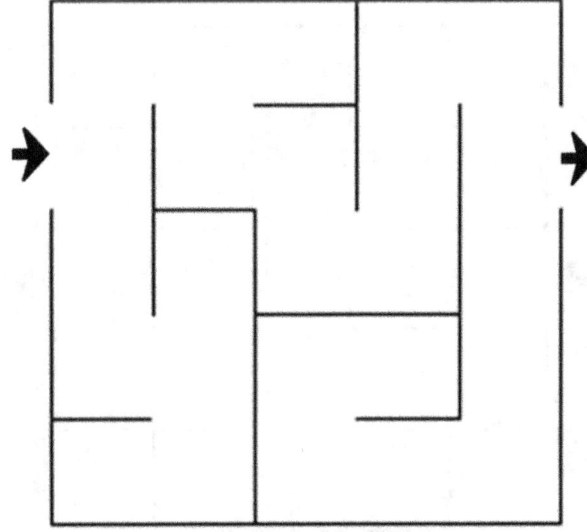

Name: ___________________   Date: _____________

15. Easy

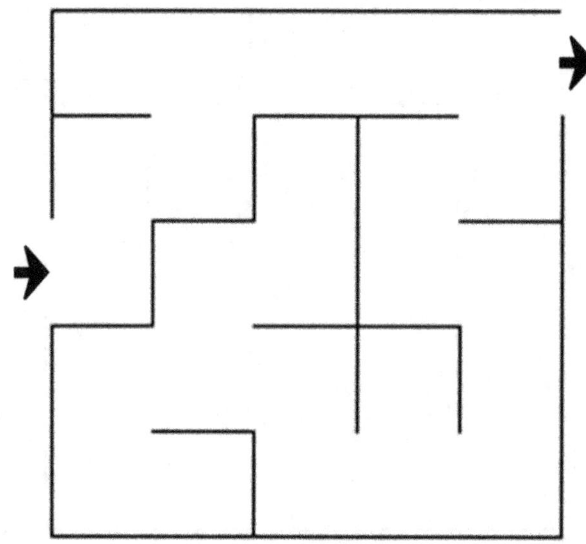

16. Easy

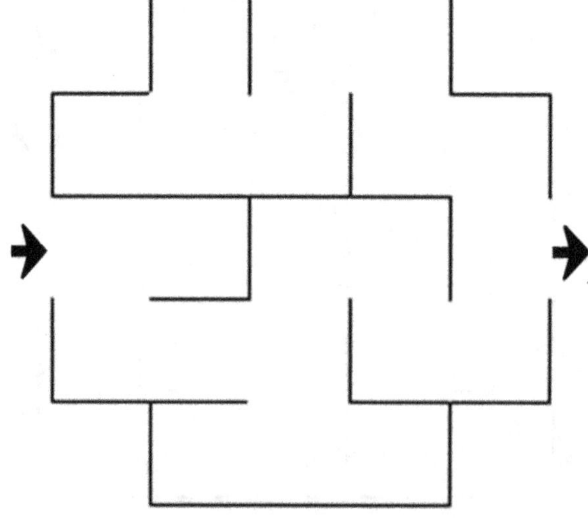

Name: _____________________   Date: _____________

17. Easy

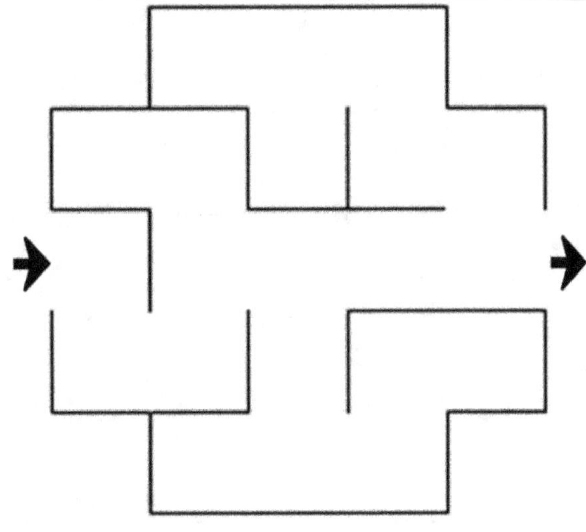

18. Easy

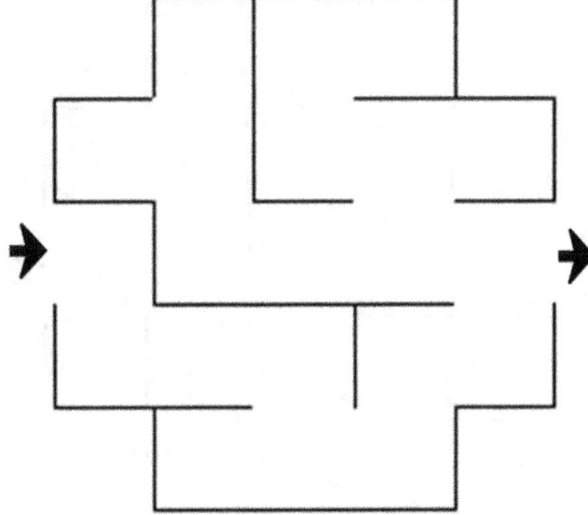

Name: ___________________   Date: _____________

19. Easy

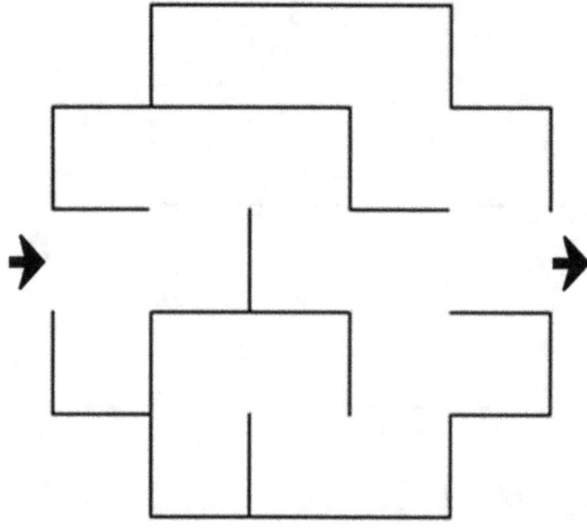

20. Easy

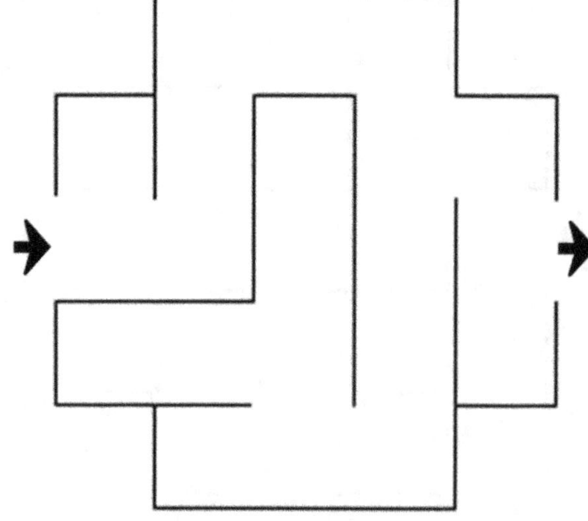

Name: ___________________   Date: ____________

21. Easy - Medium

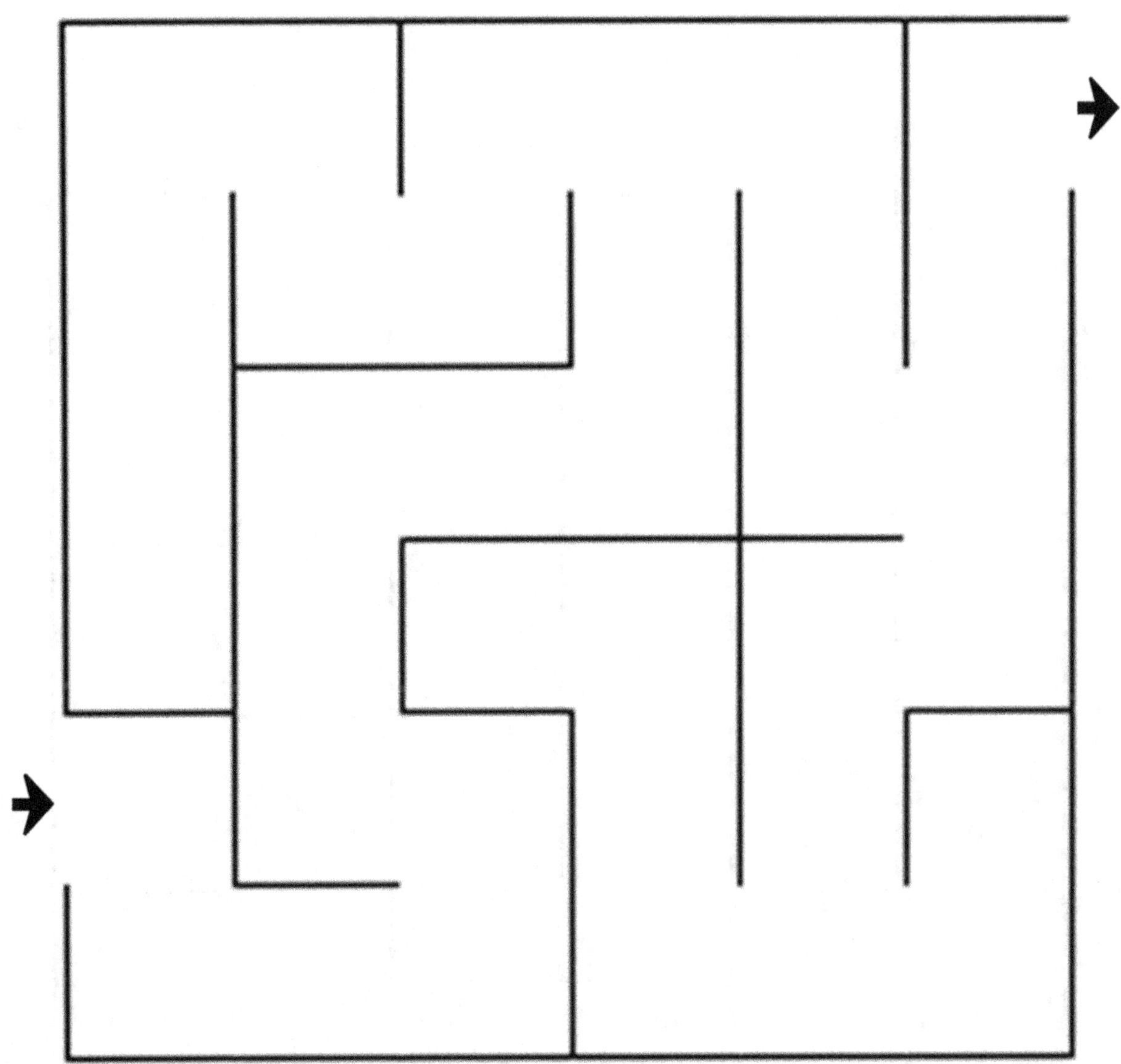

Name: _____________________   Date: _____________

22. Easy - Medium

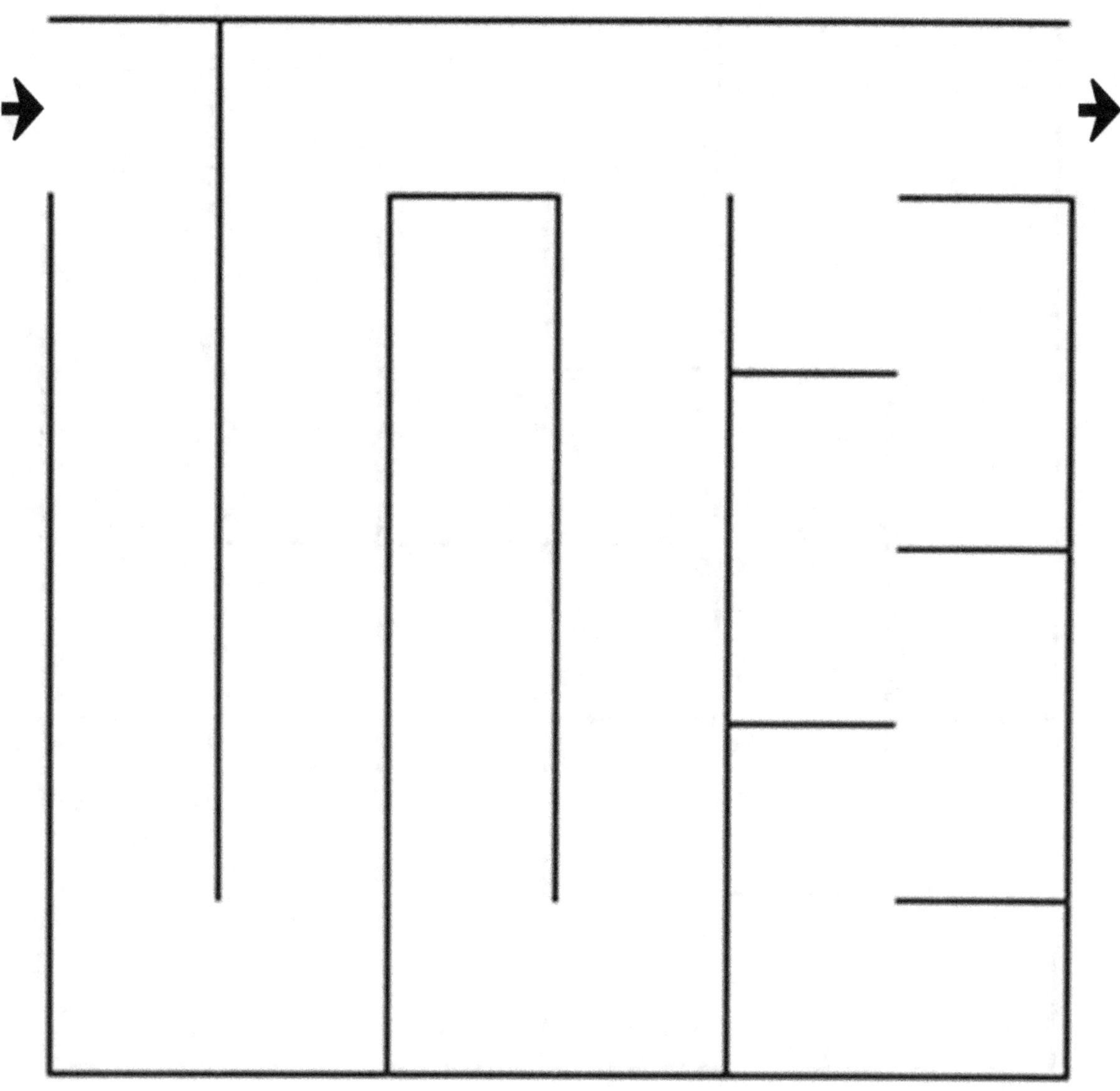

Name: _________________________   Date: _____________

23. Easy - Medium

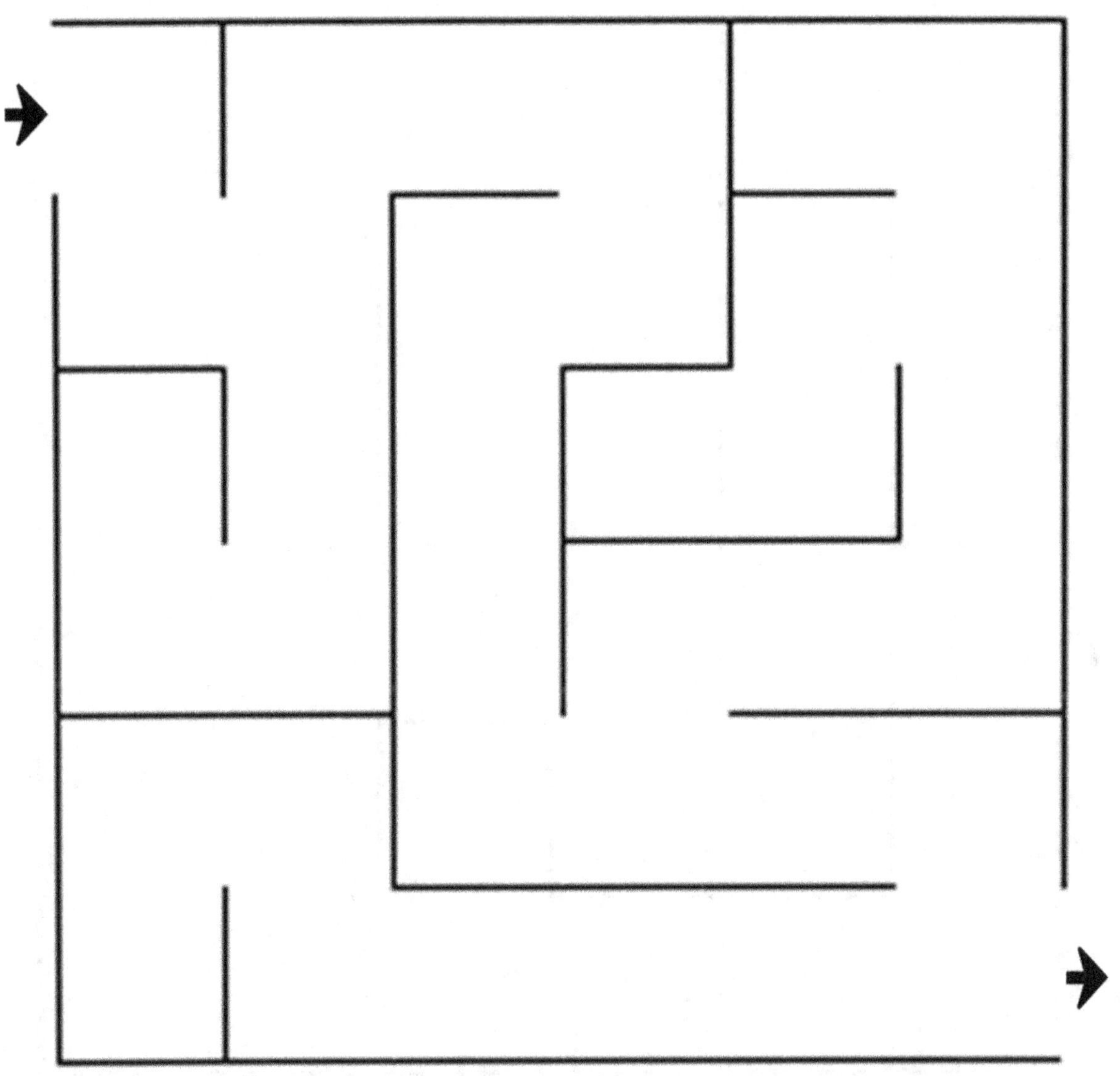

Name: ___________________   Date: _____________

24. Easy - Medium

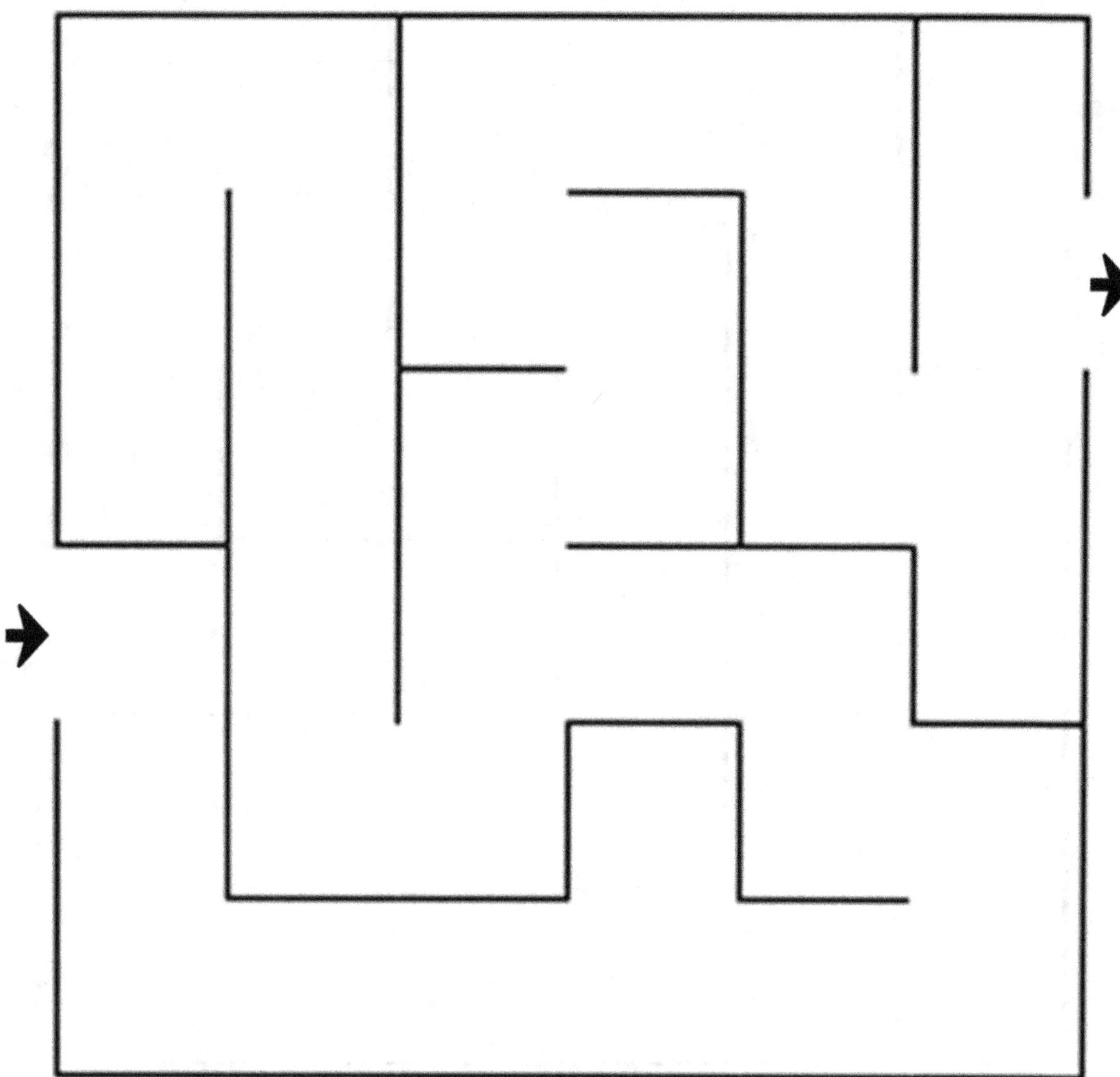

Name: _________________________   Date: _____________

25. Easy - Medium

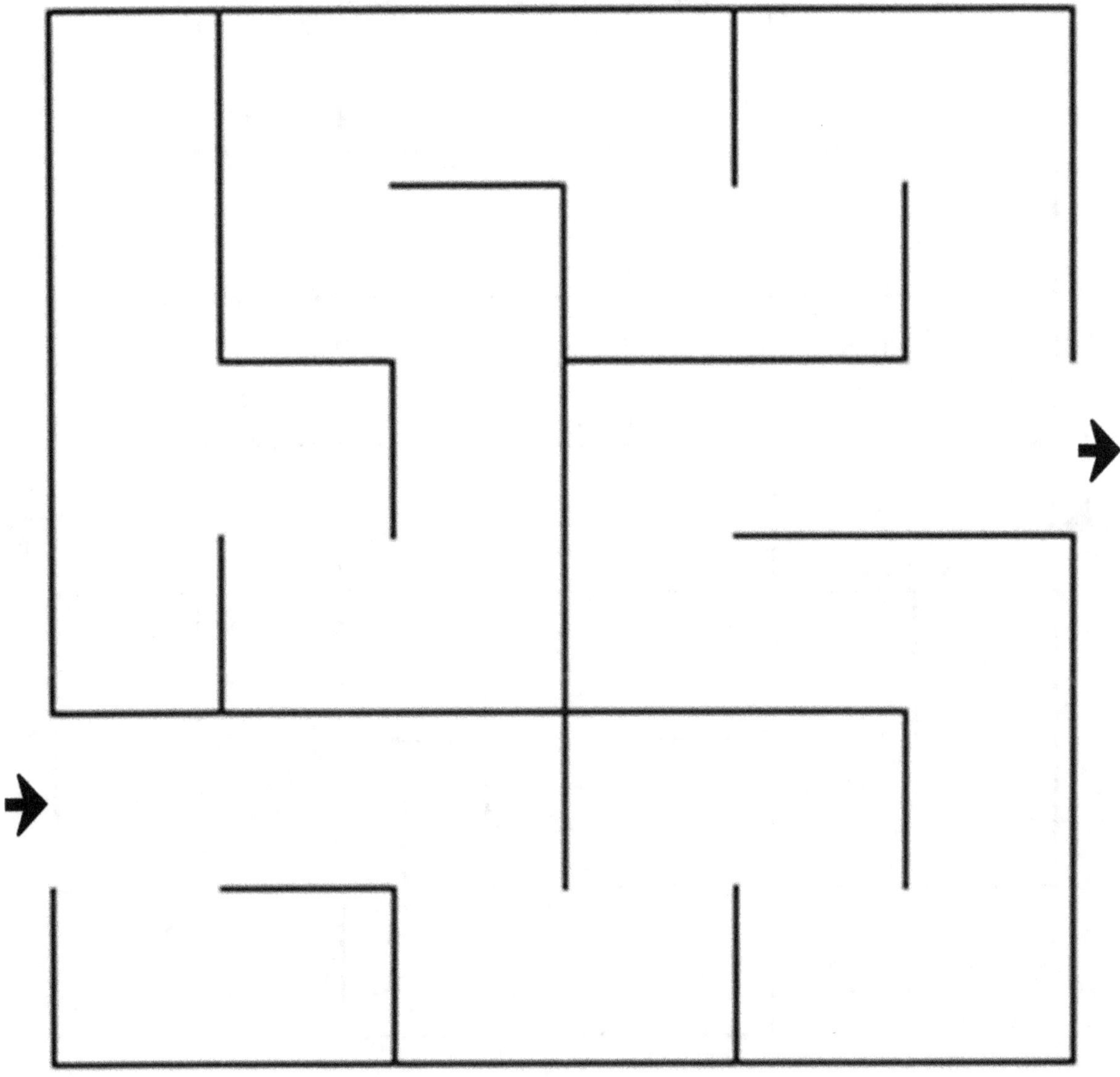

Name: _________________________   Date: _____________

26. Easy - Medium

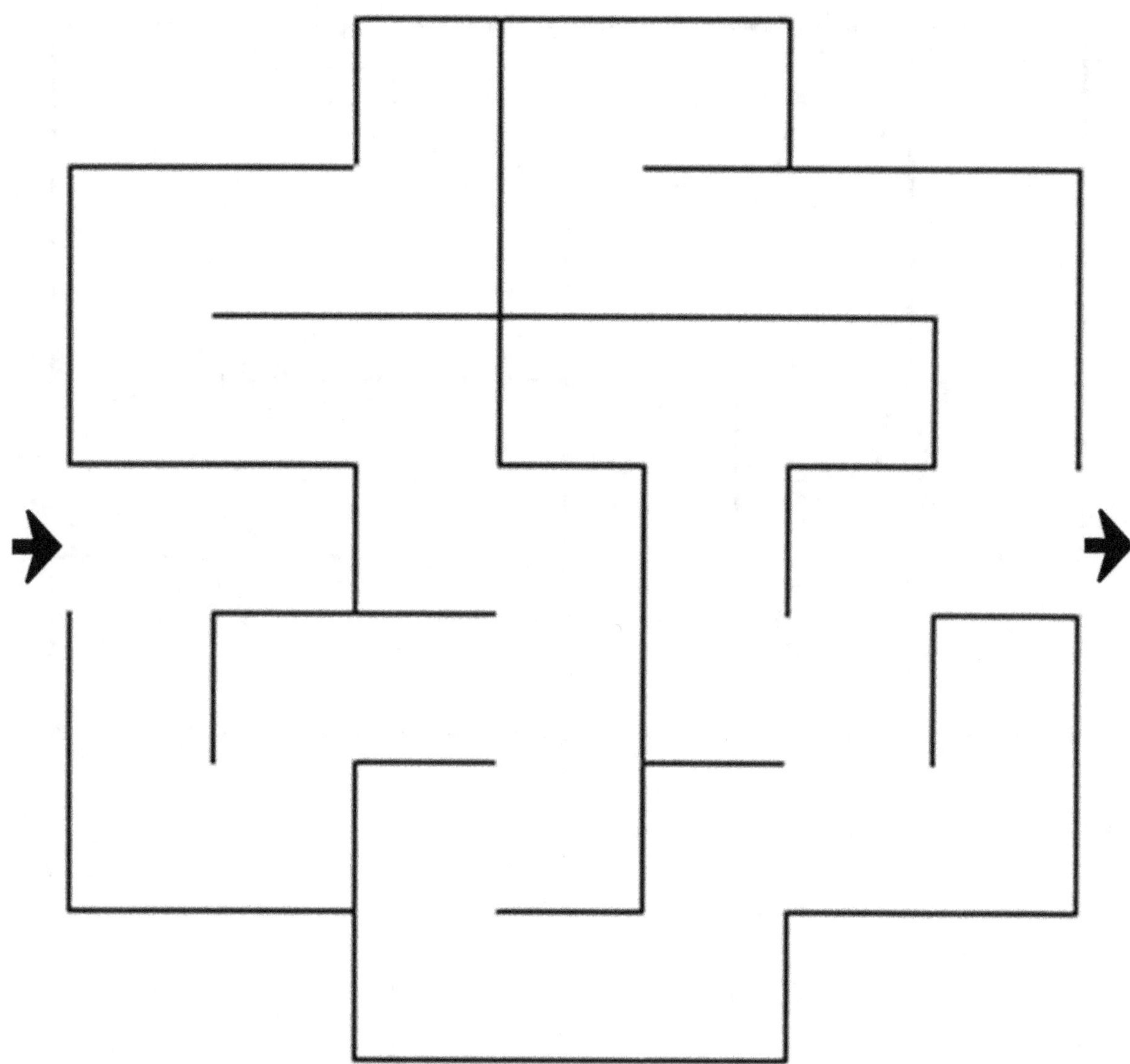

Name: ___________________   Date: ______________

27. Easy - Medium

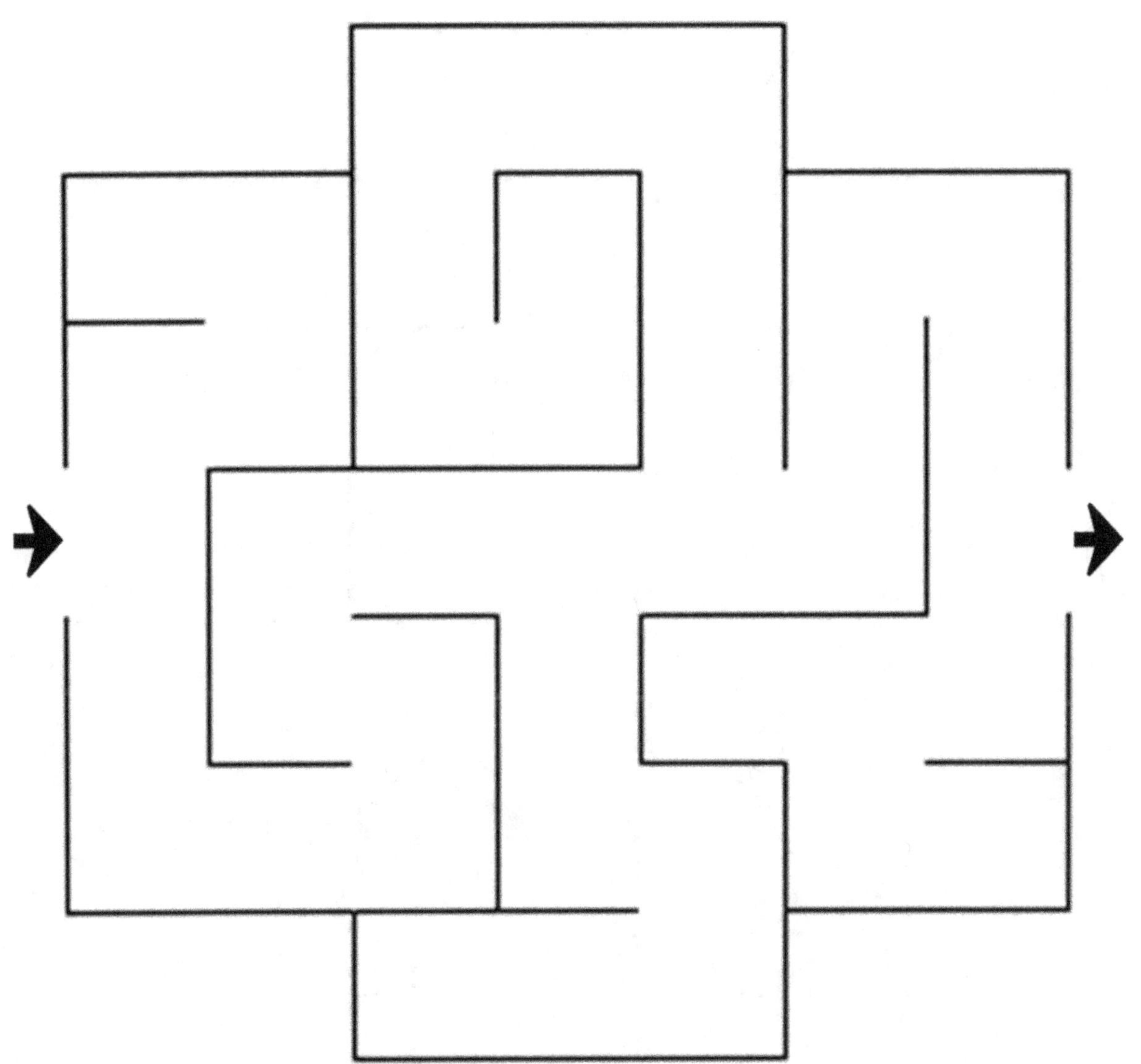

Name: _________________________ Date: _______________

28. Easy - Medium

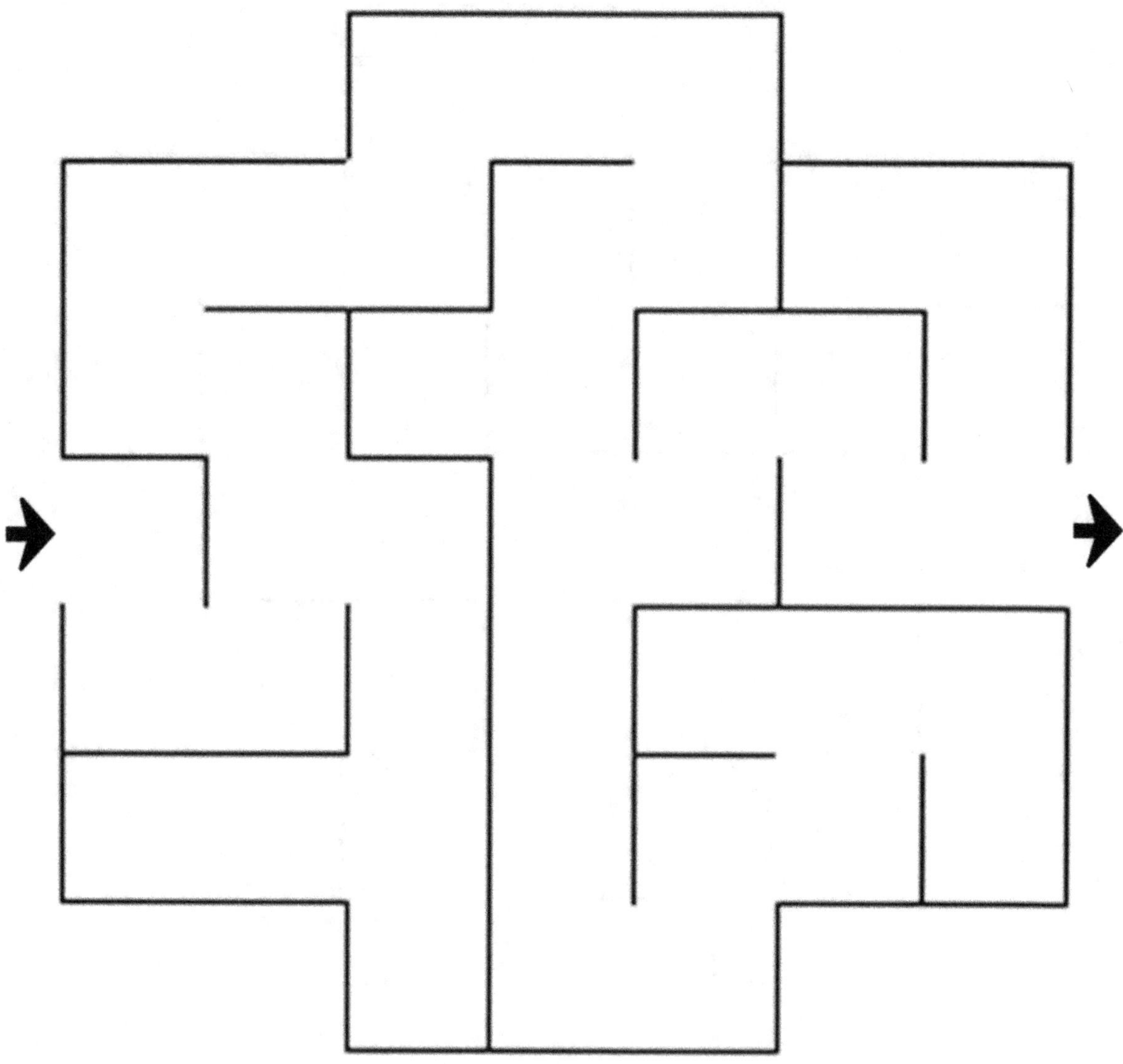

Name: _________________________   Date: ______________

29. Easy - Medium

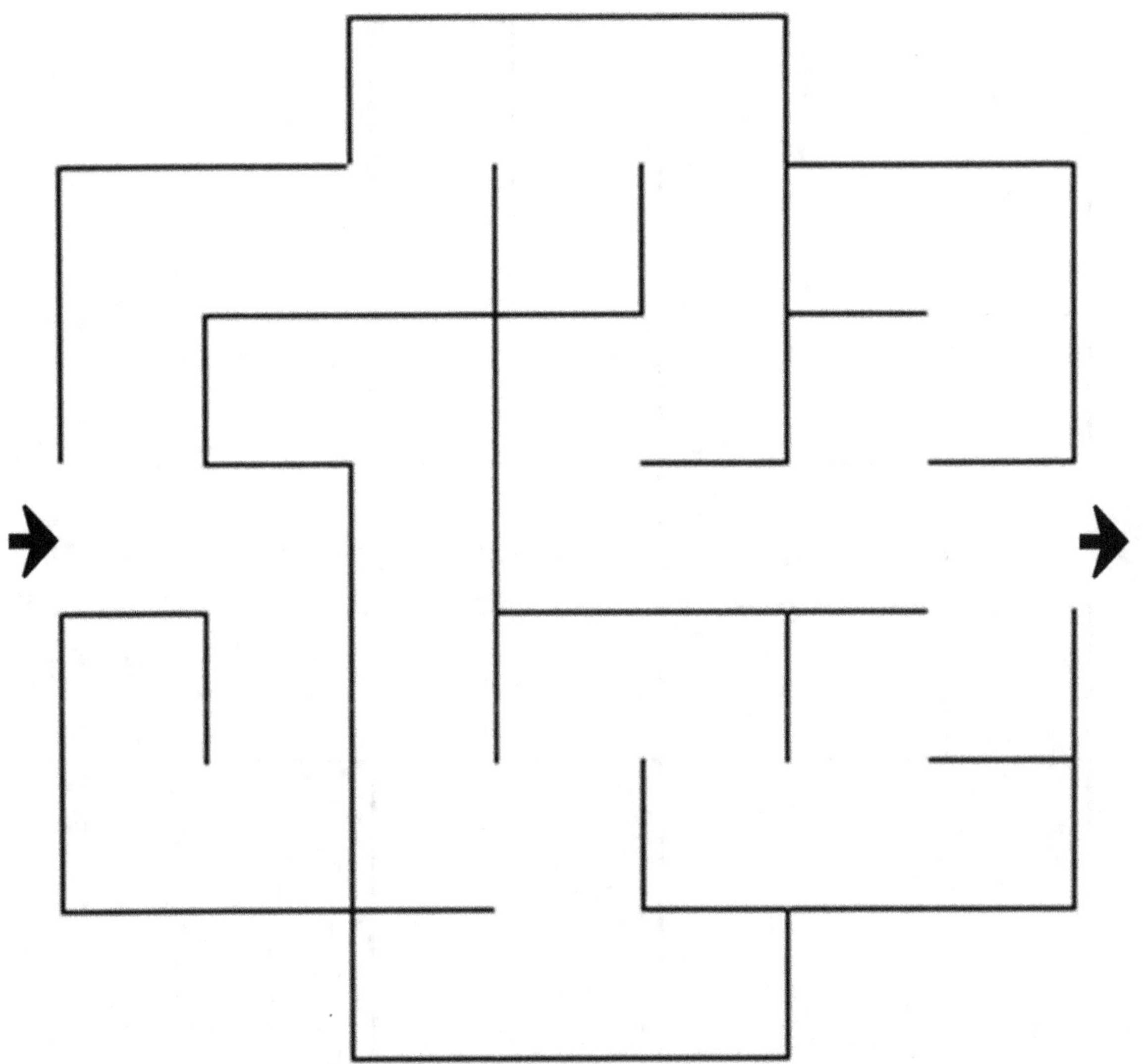

Name: ________________________   Date: ____________

30. Easy - Medium

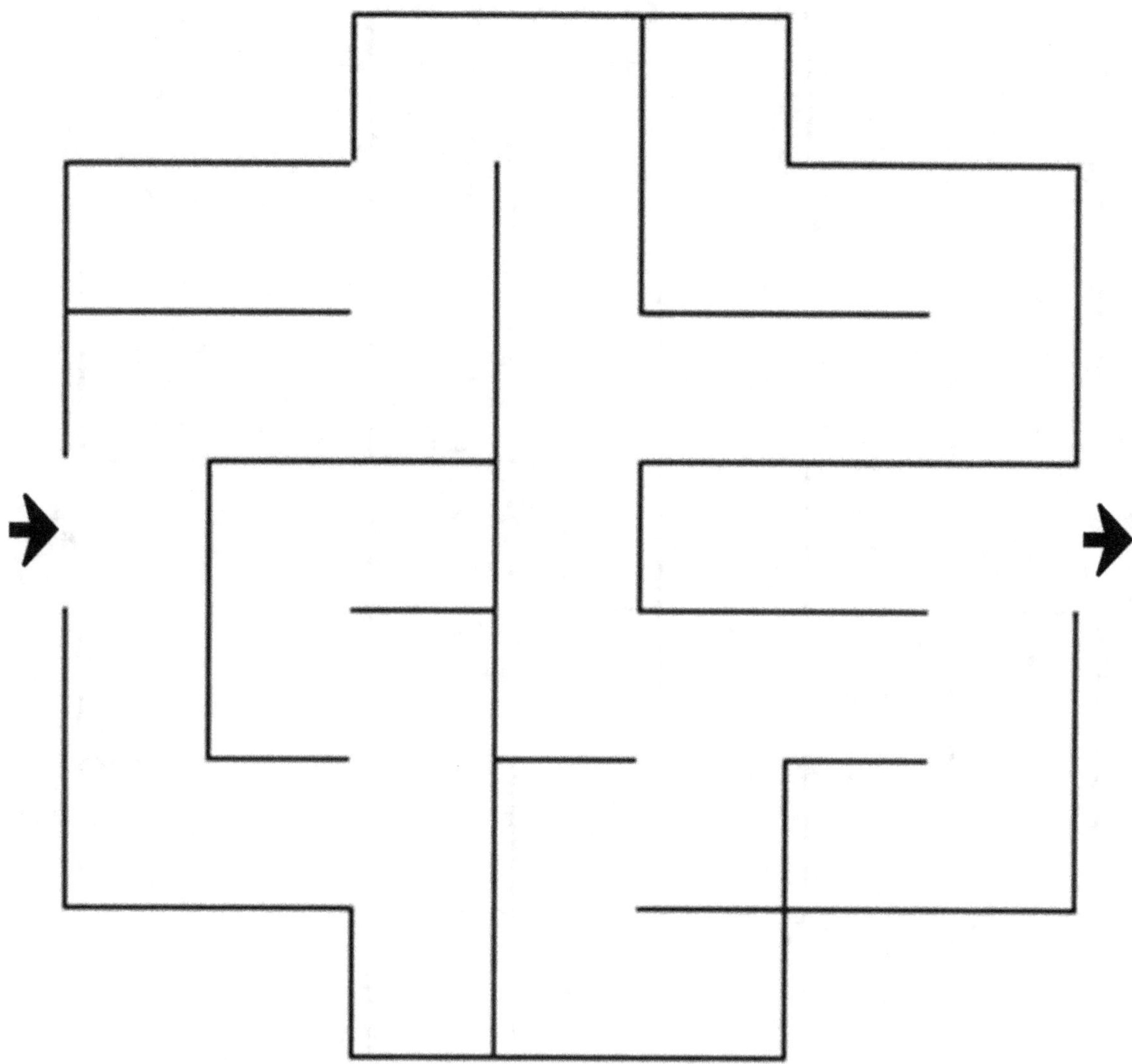

Name: _________________________   Date: _____________

31. Medium

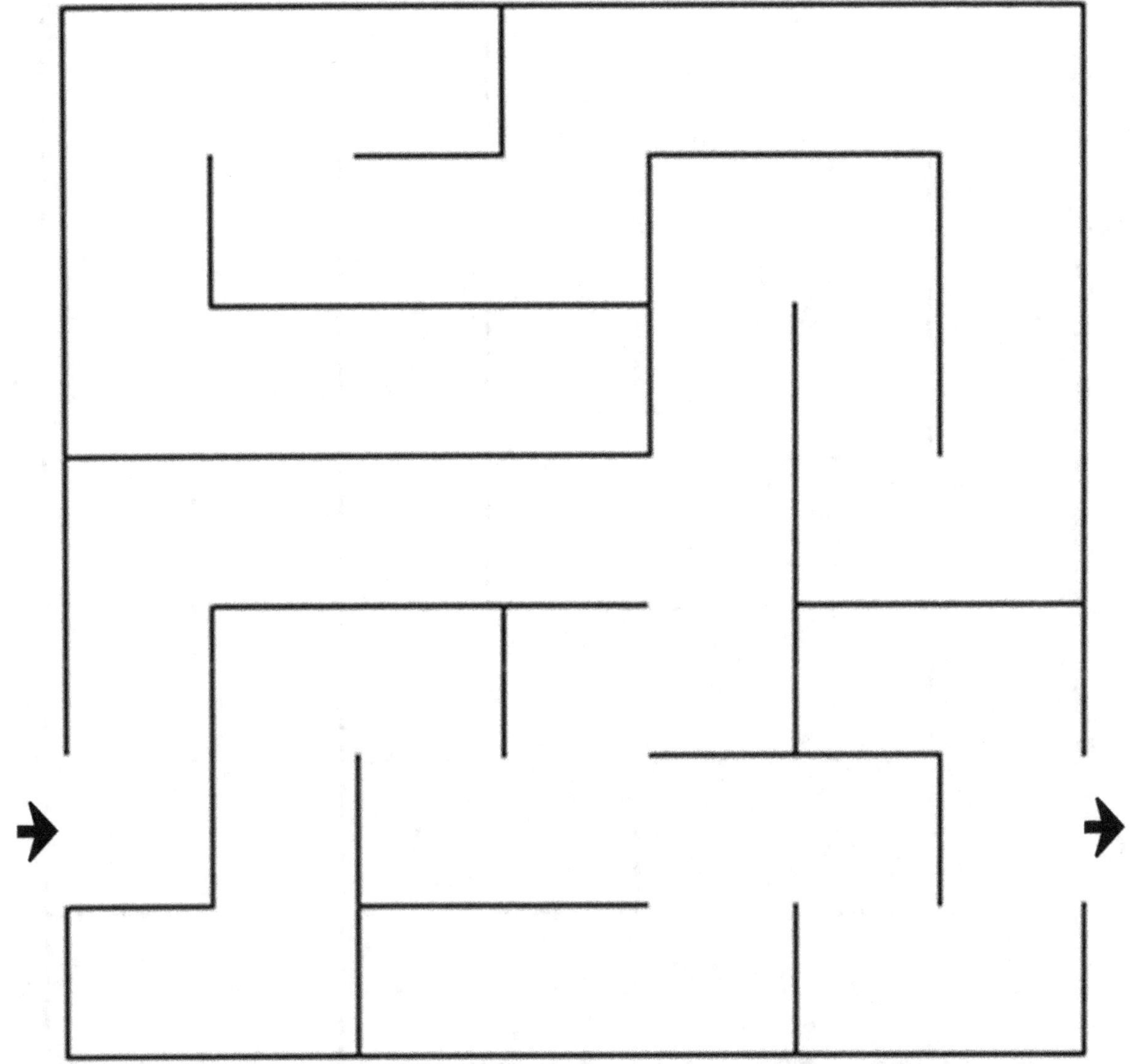

Name: ___________________   Date: ___________

32. Medium

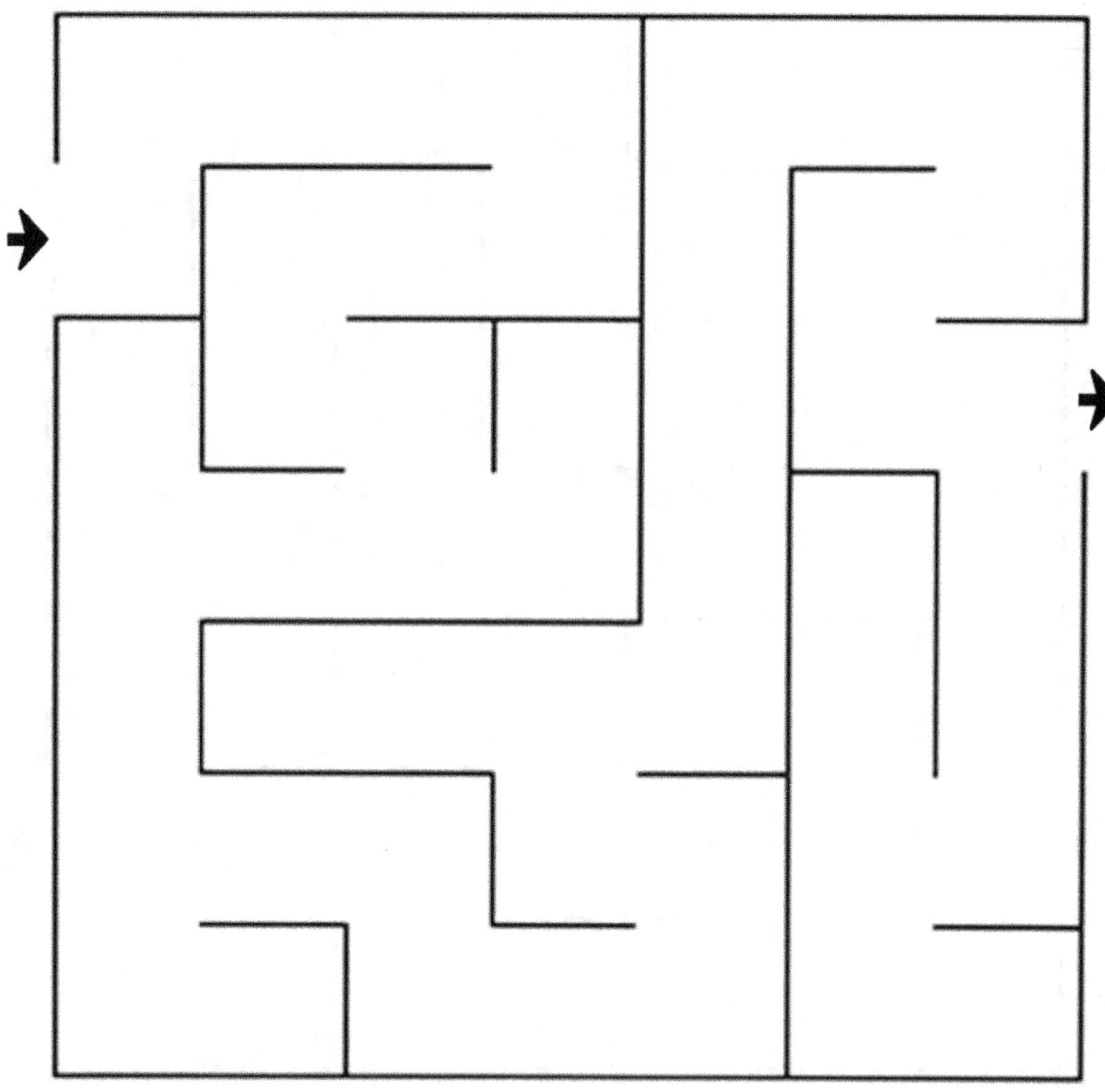

Kindergarten Mazes

Name: _________________________   Date: _______________

33. Medium

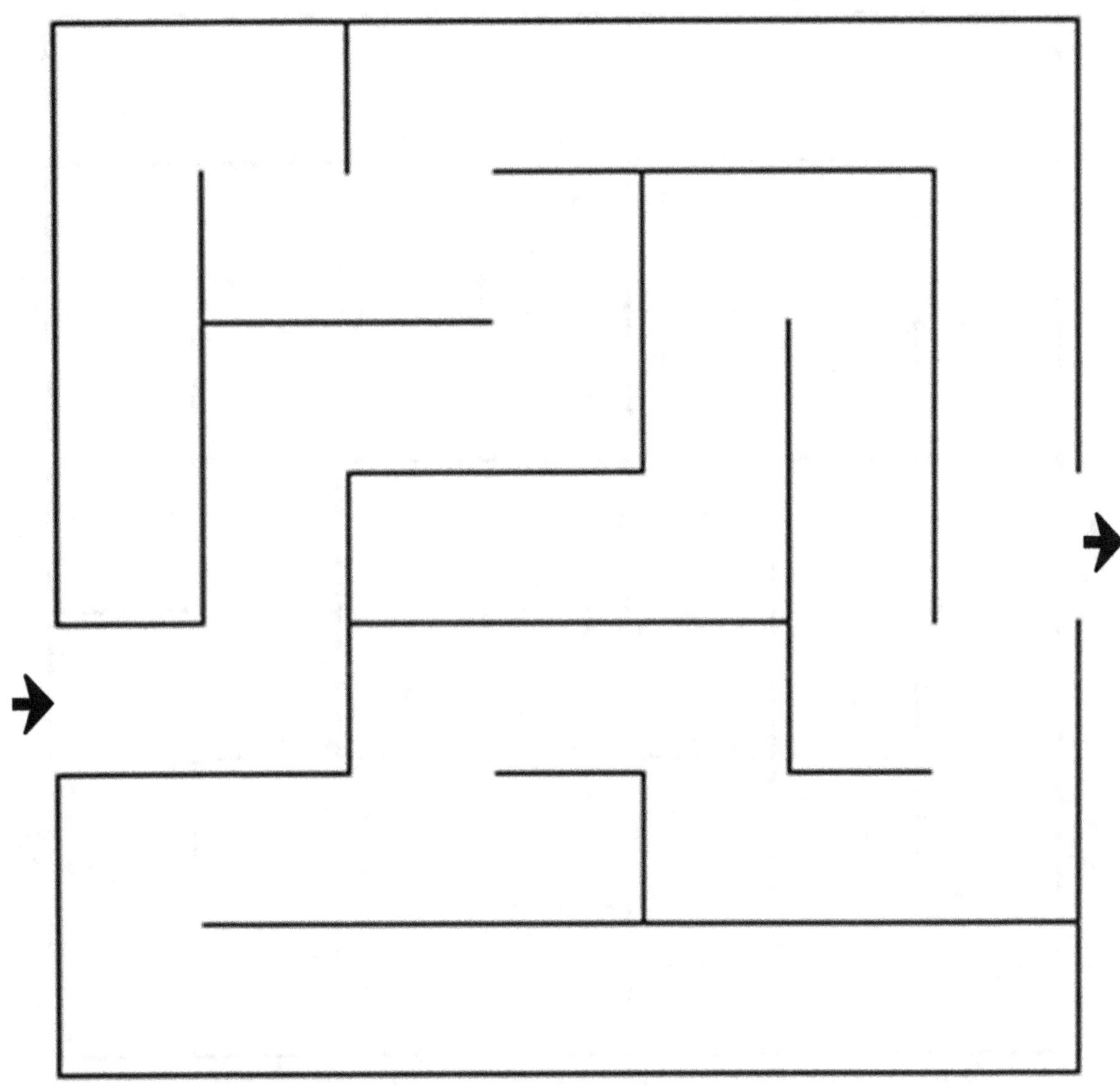

Name: _____________________ Date: _____________

34. Medium

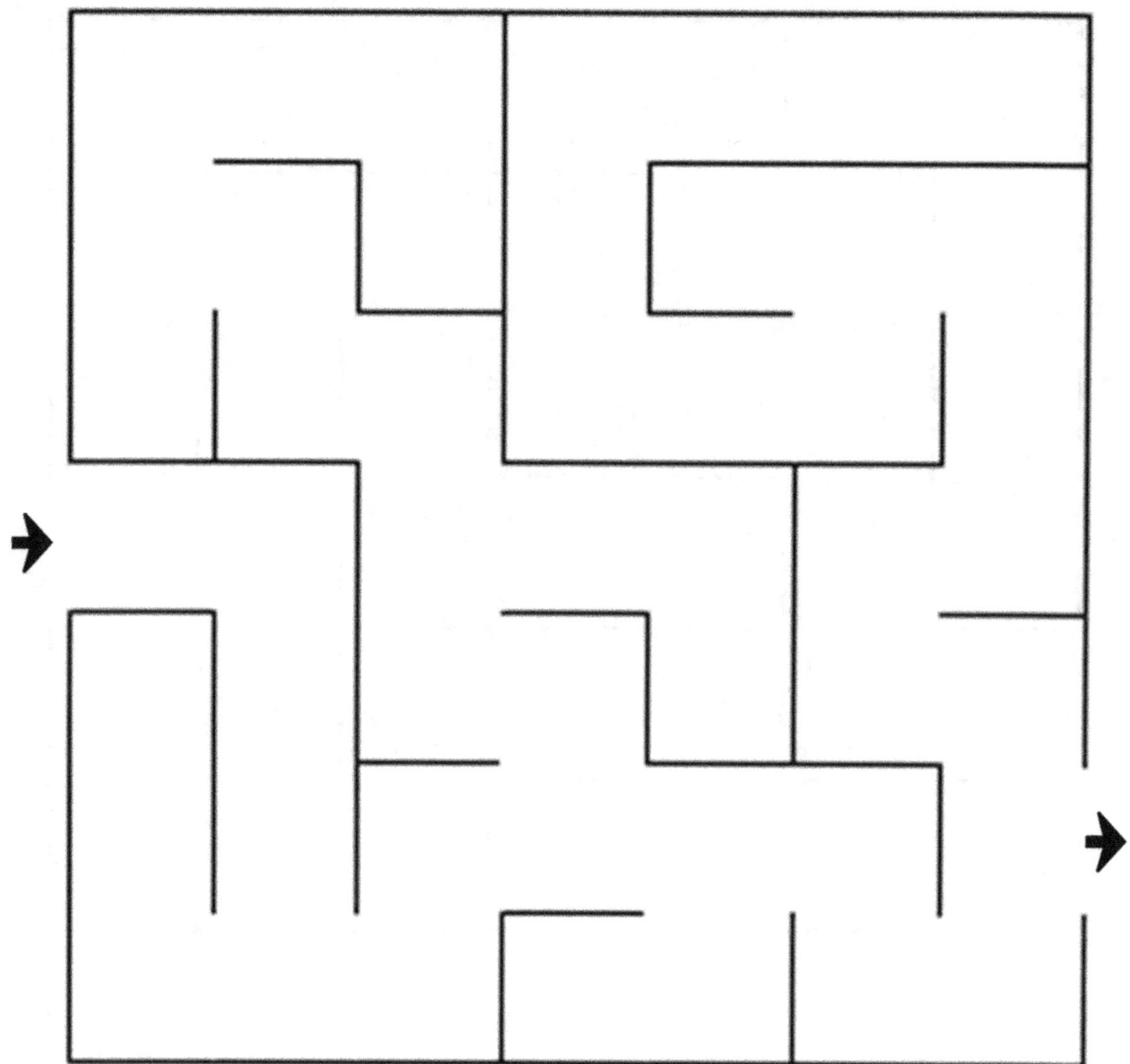

Kindergarten Mazes

Name: ________________________   Date: ____________

35. Medium

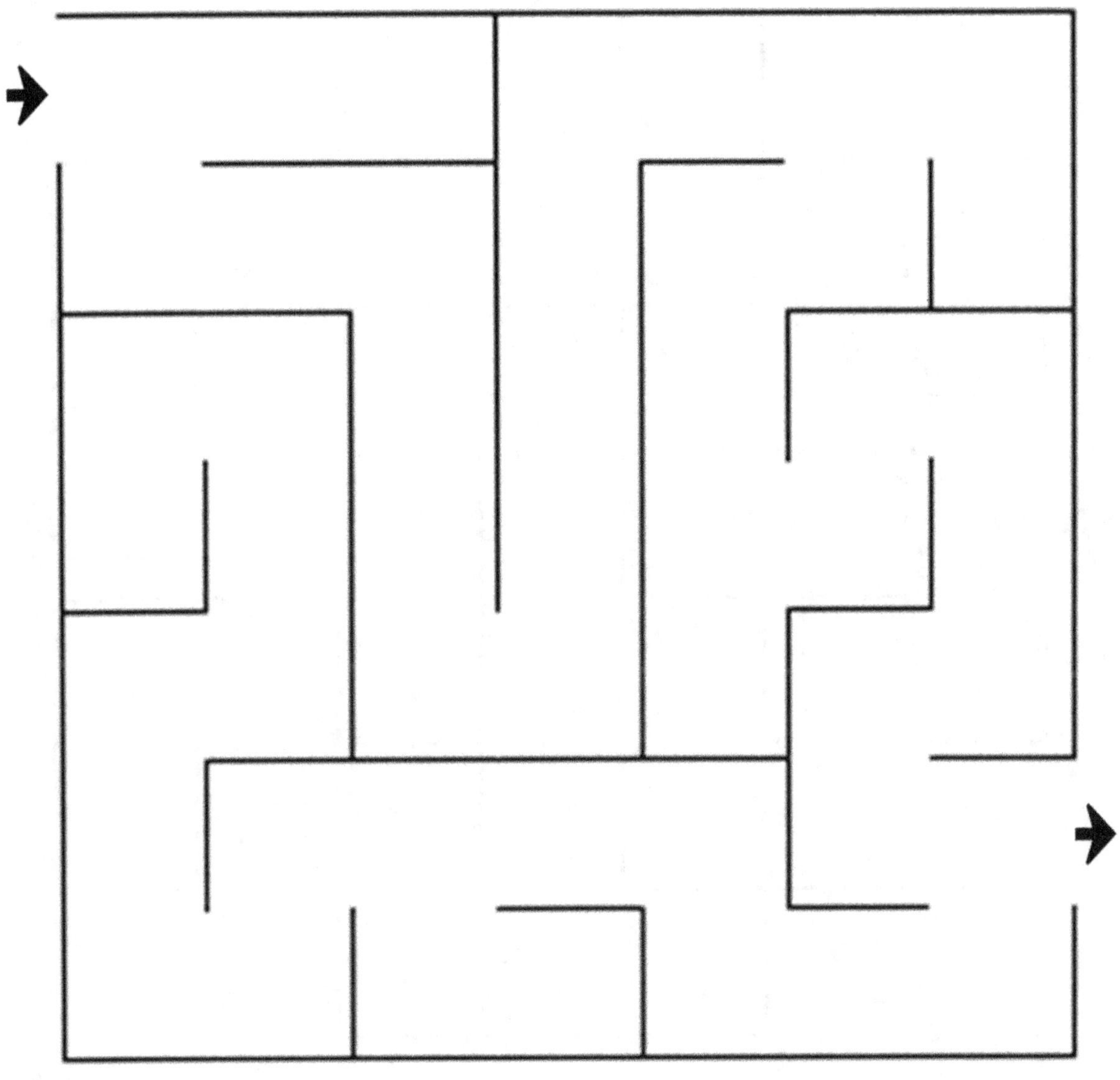

Name: _________________ Date: _____________

36. Medium

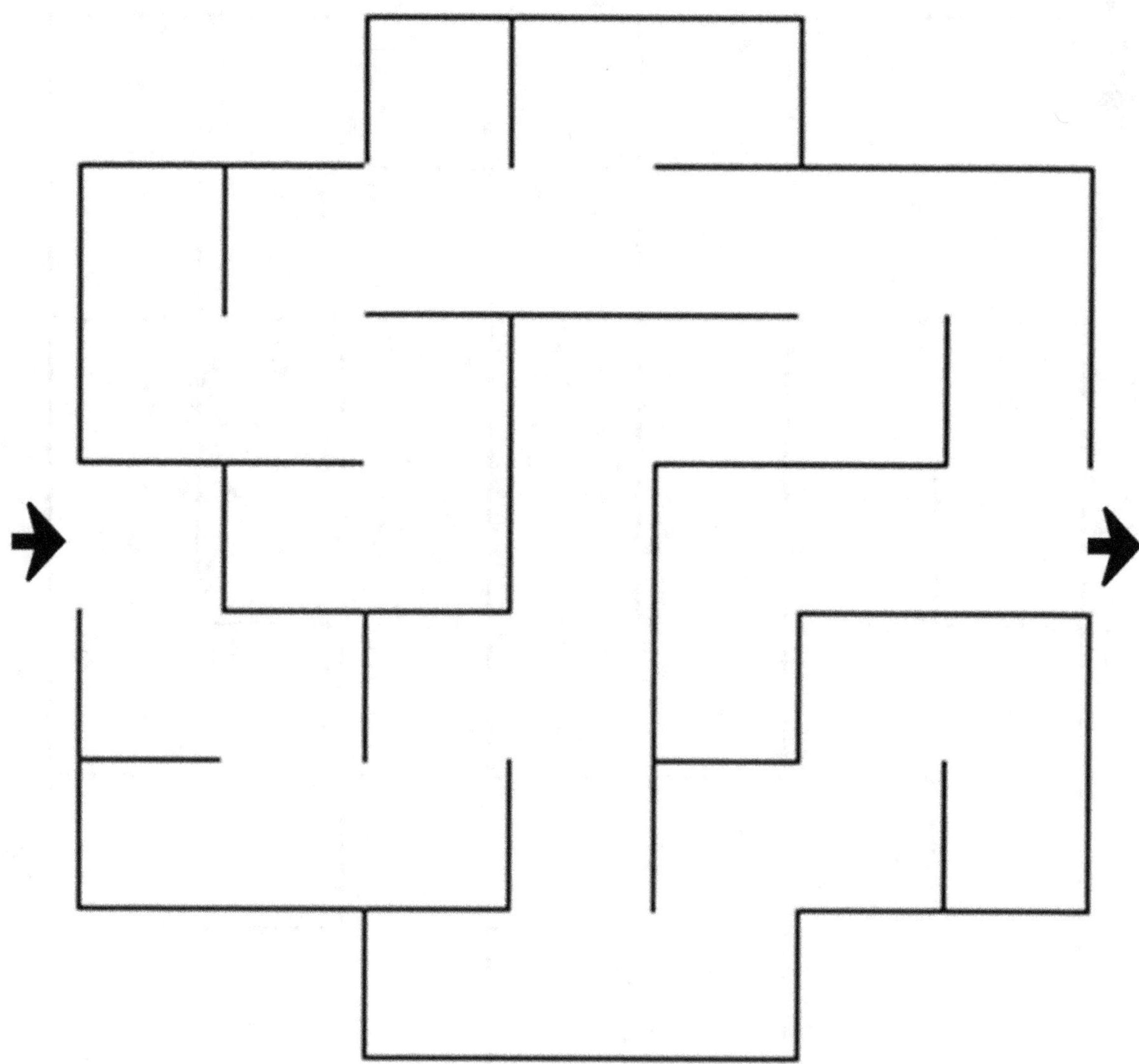

Kindergarten Mazes

Name: _______________________   Date: ____________

37. Medium

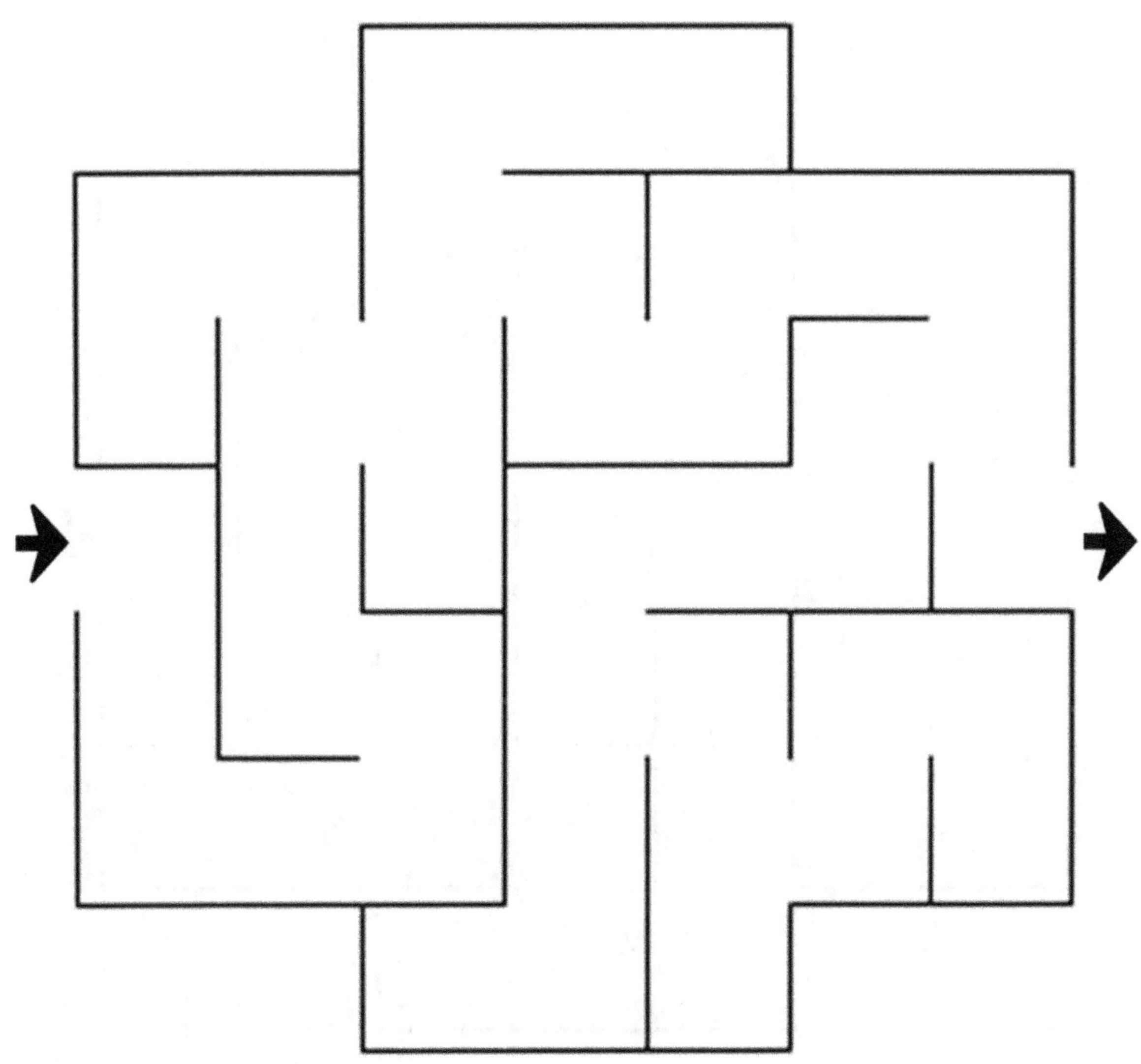

Name: _______________________ Date: _______________

38. Medium

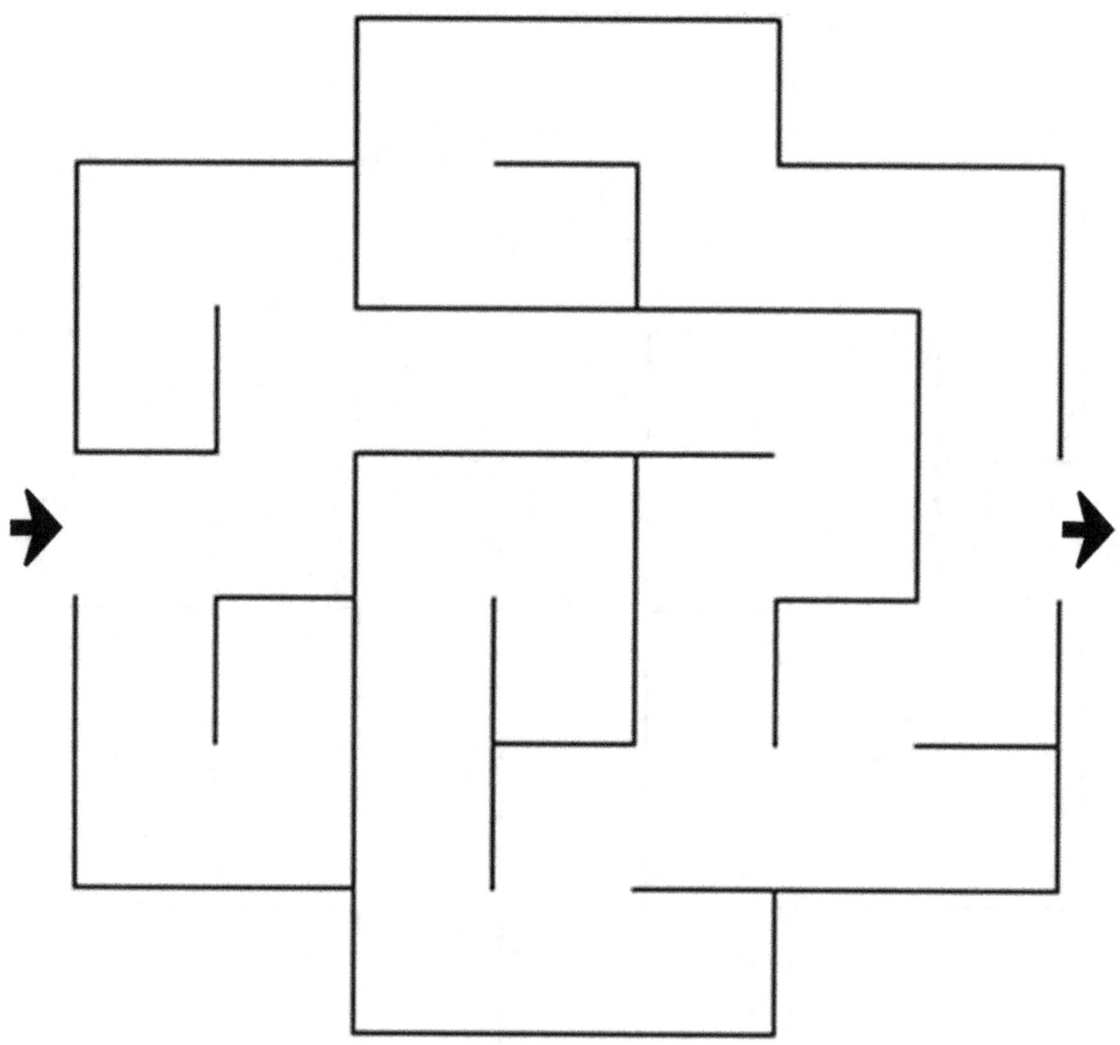

Kindergarten Mazes

Name: _____________________   Date: _____________

39. Medium

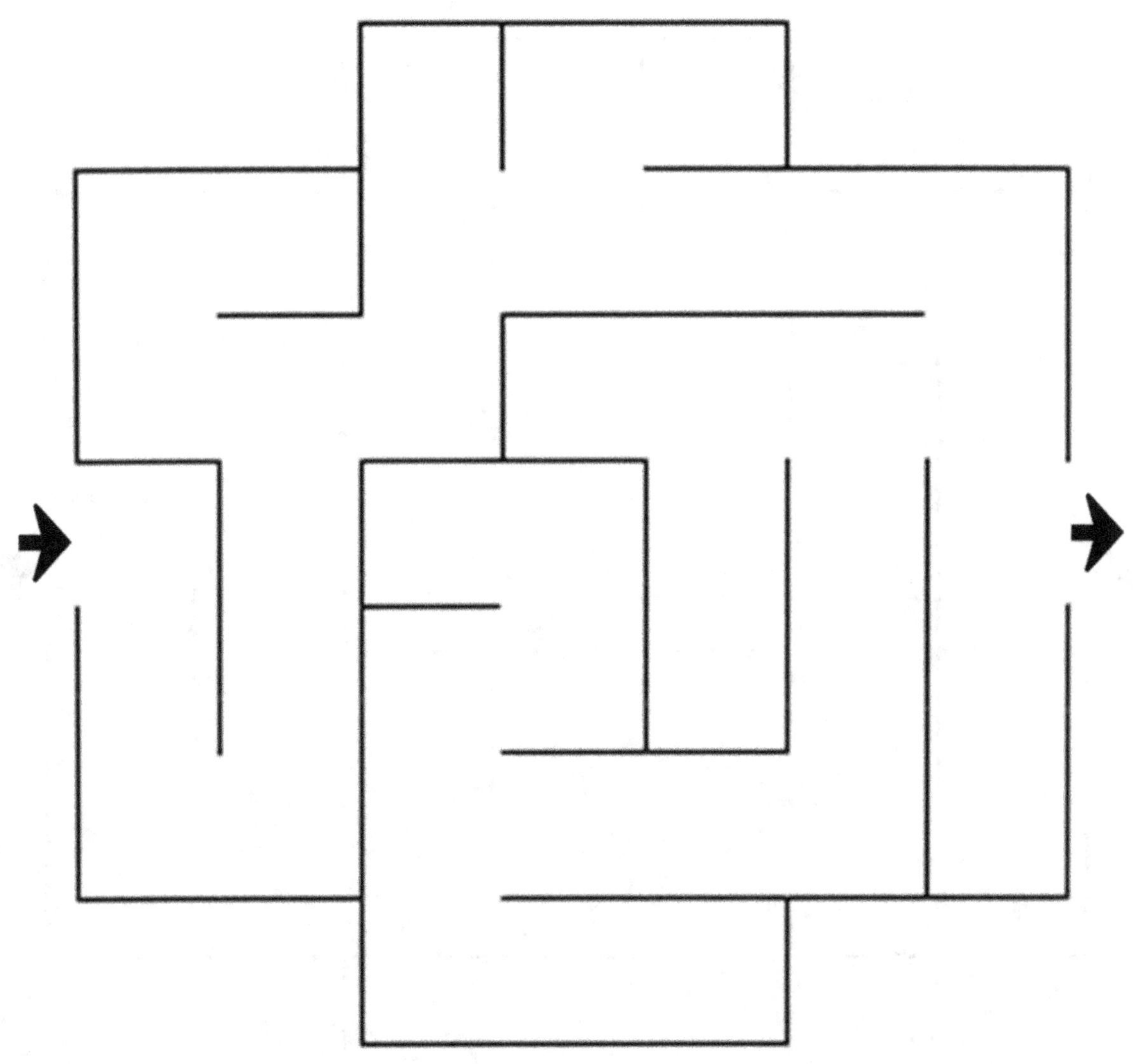

Name: ___________________   Date: ______________

40. Medium

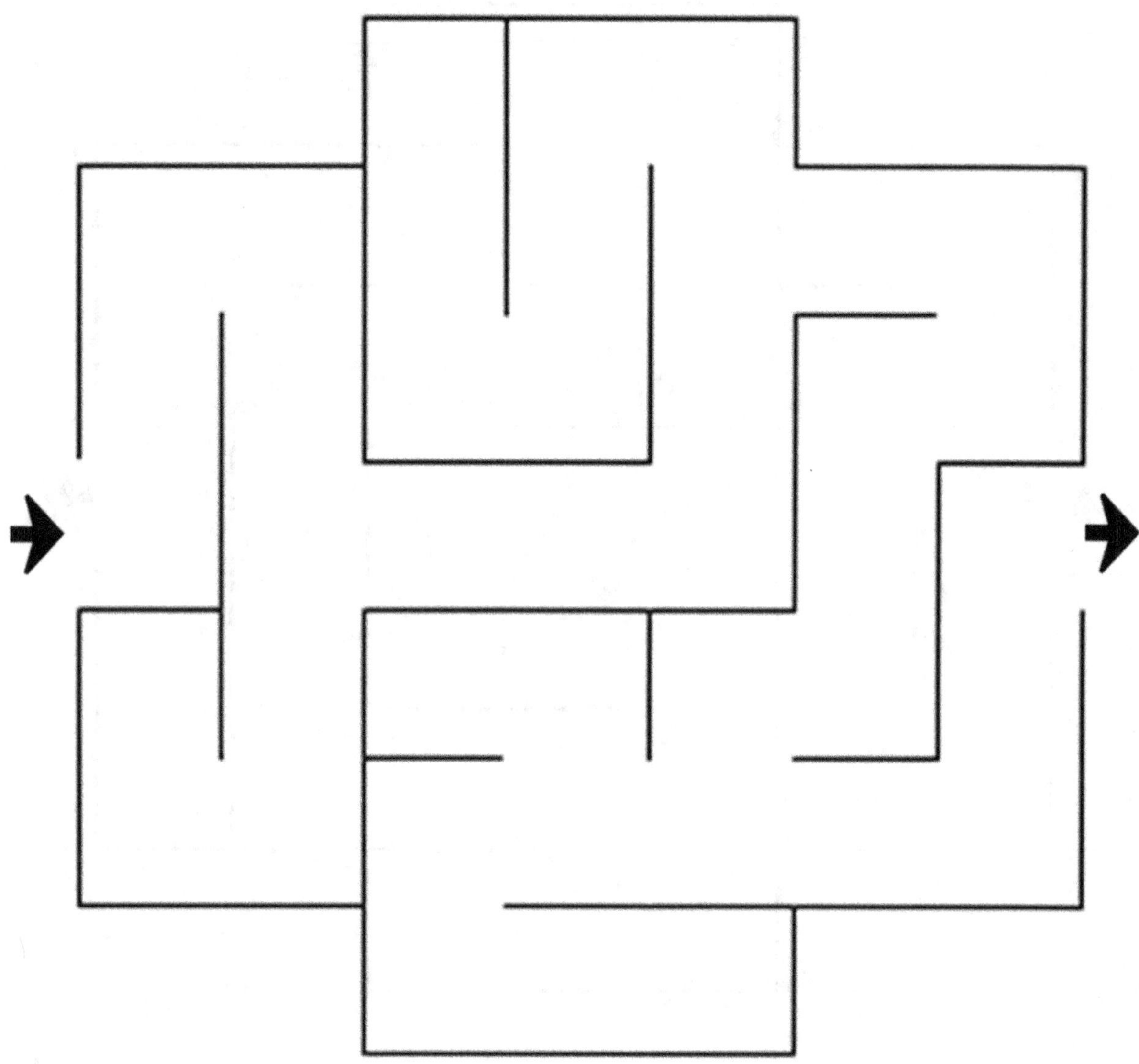

Name: _________________________   Date: ______________

41. Medium

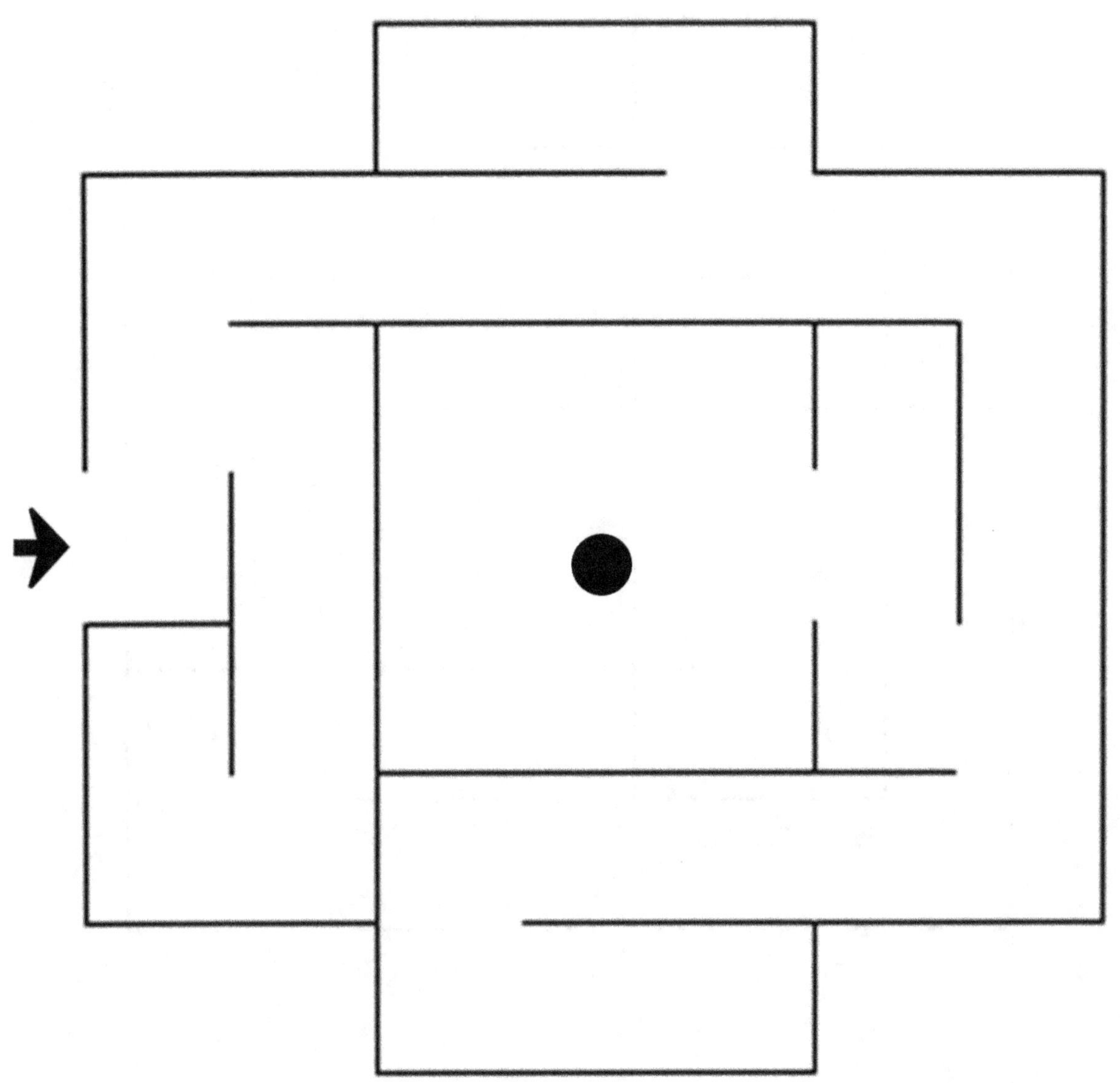

Name: _________________________   Date: _______________

42. Medium

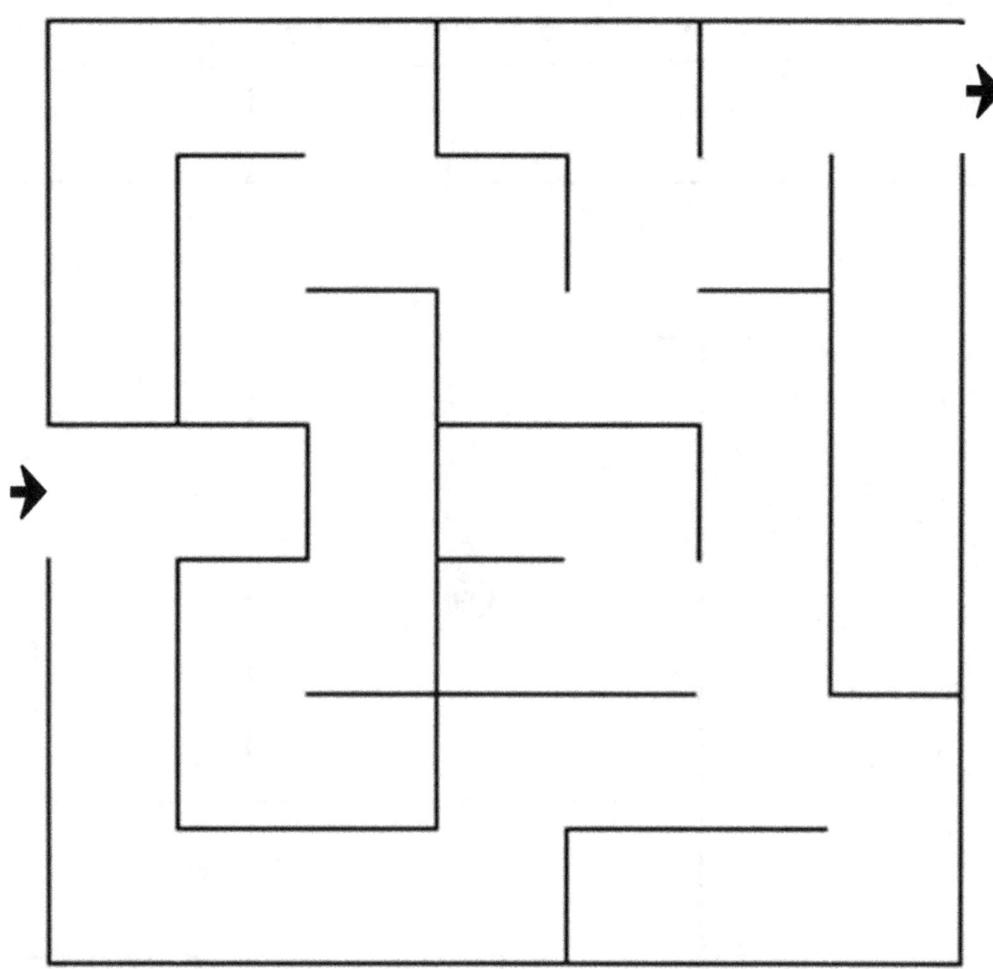

Name: _______________________ Date: _____________

43. Medium - Difficult

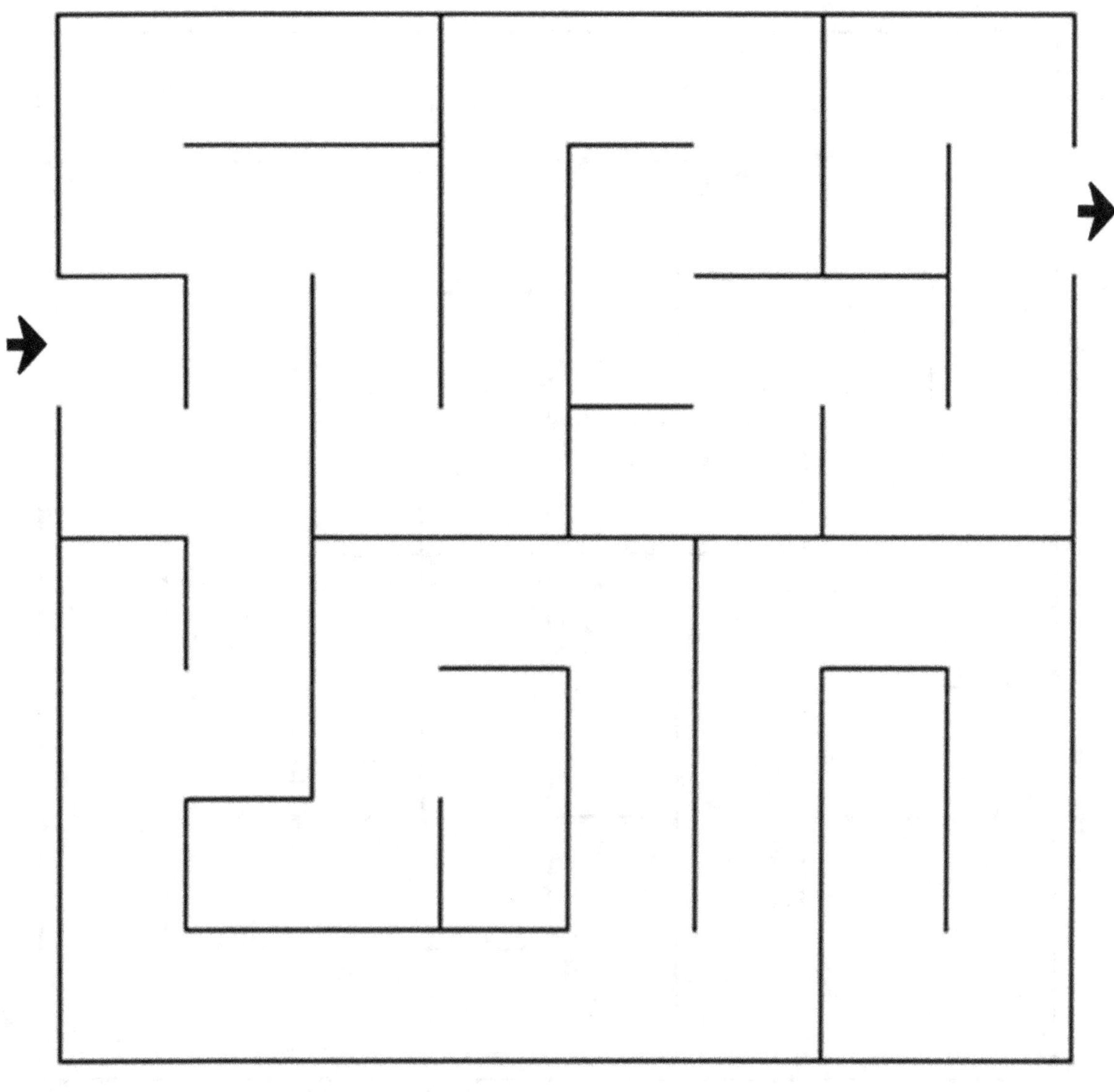

Name: _______________________

Date: _____________

44. Medium - Difficult

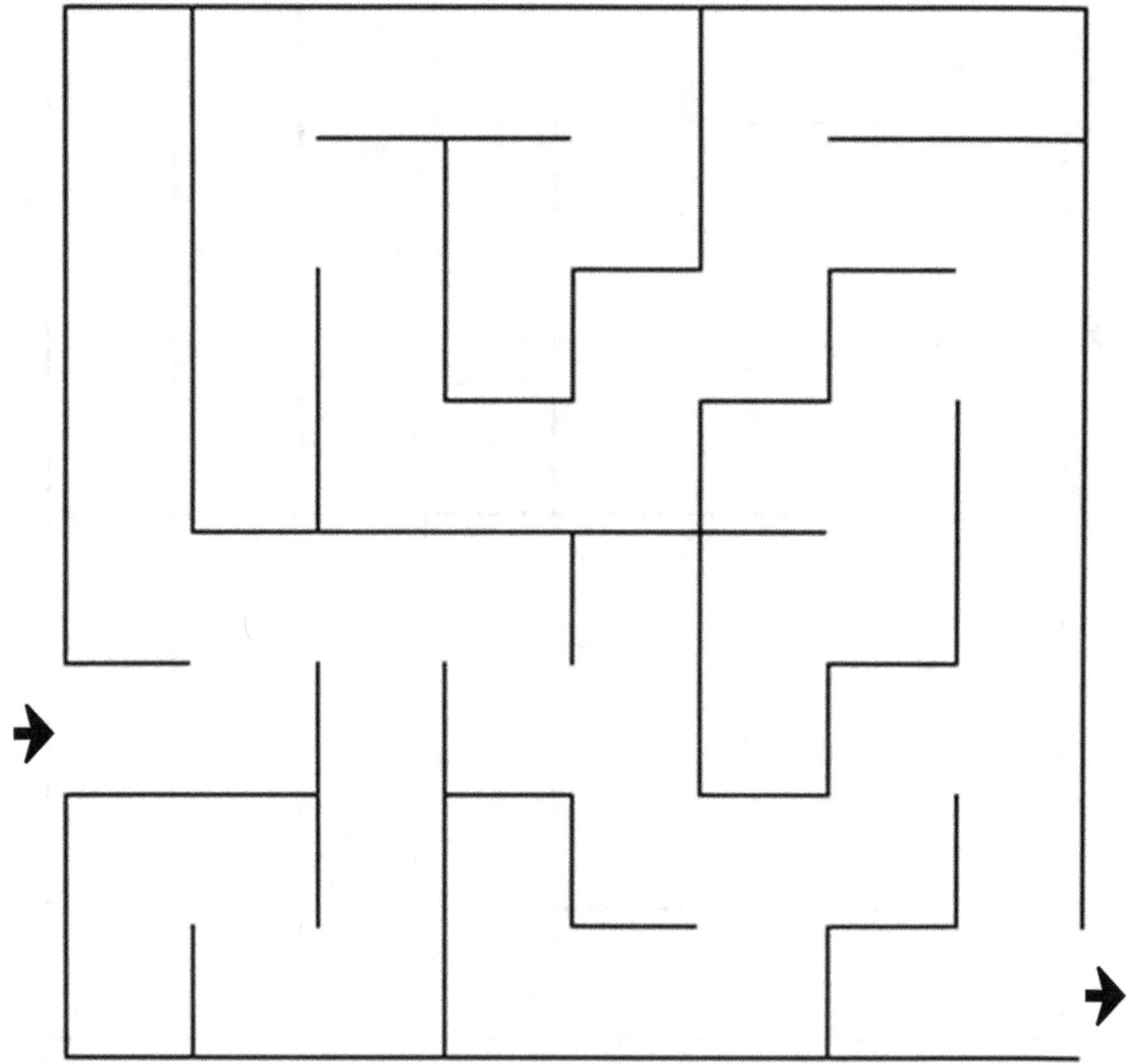

Name: __________________   Date: ______________

45. Medium - Difficult

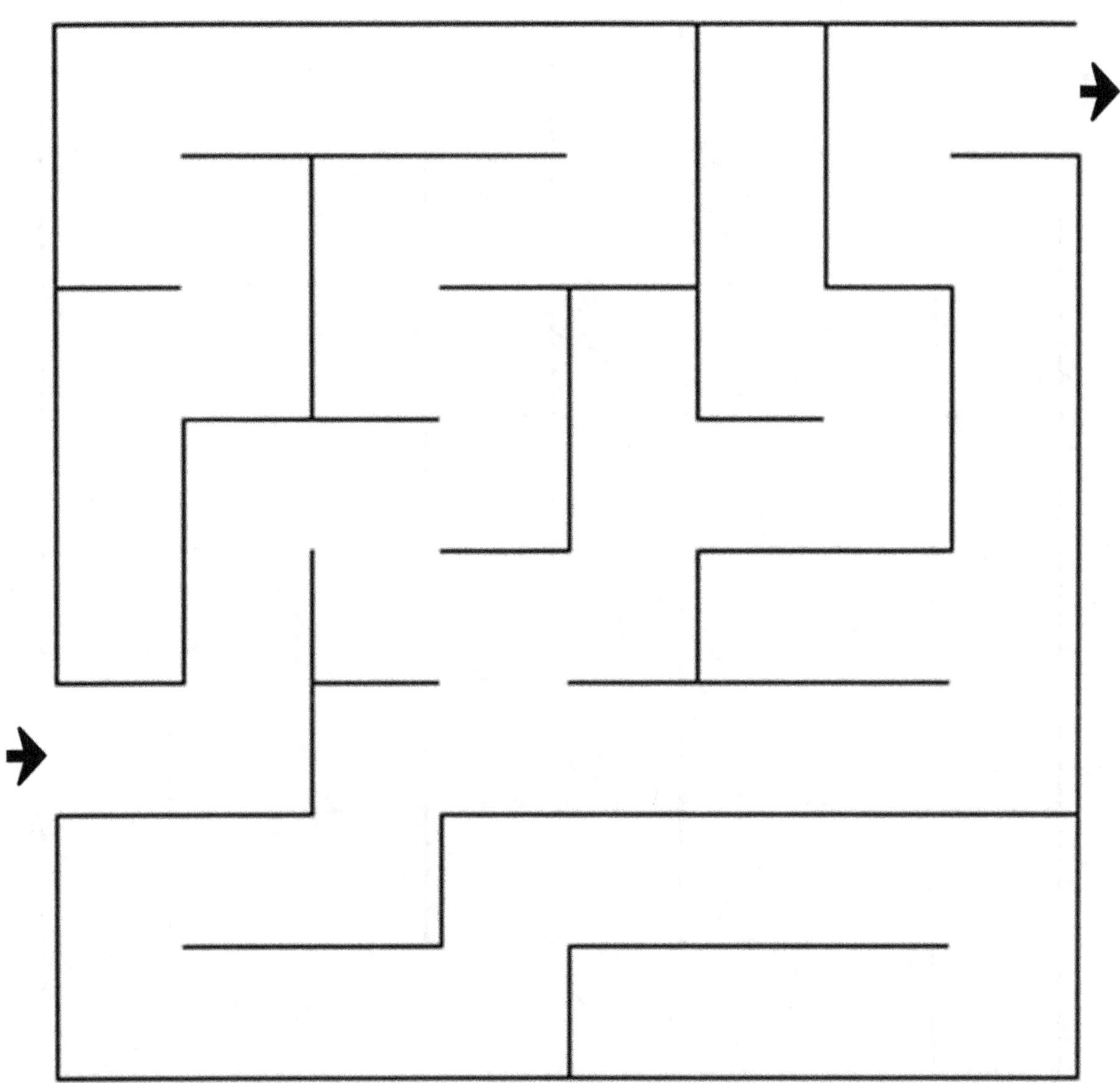

Name: ___________________   Date: ______________

46. Medium - Difficult

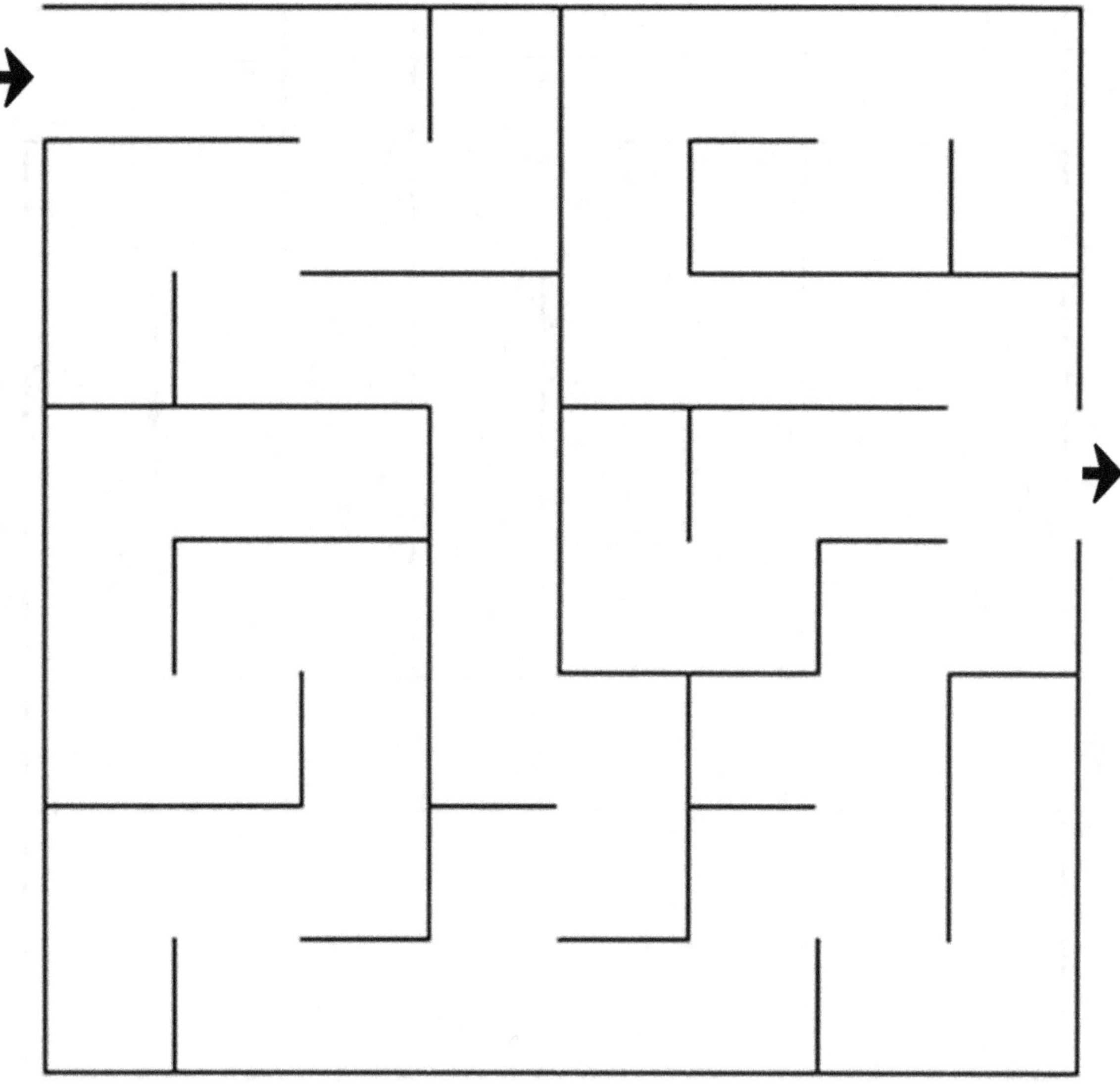

Name: ___________________   Date: ______________

47. Medium - Difficult

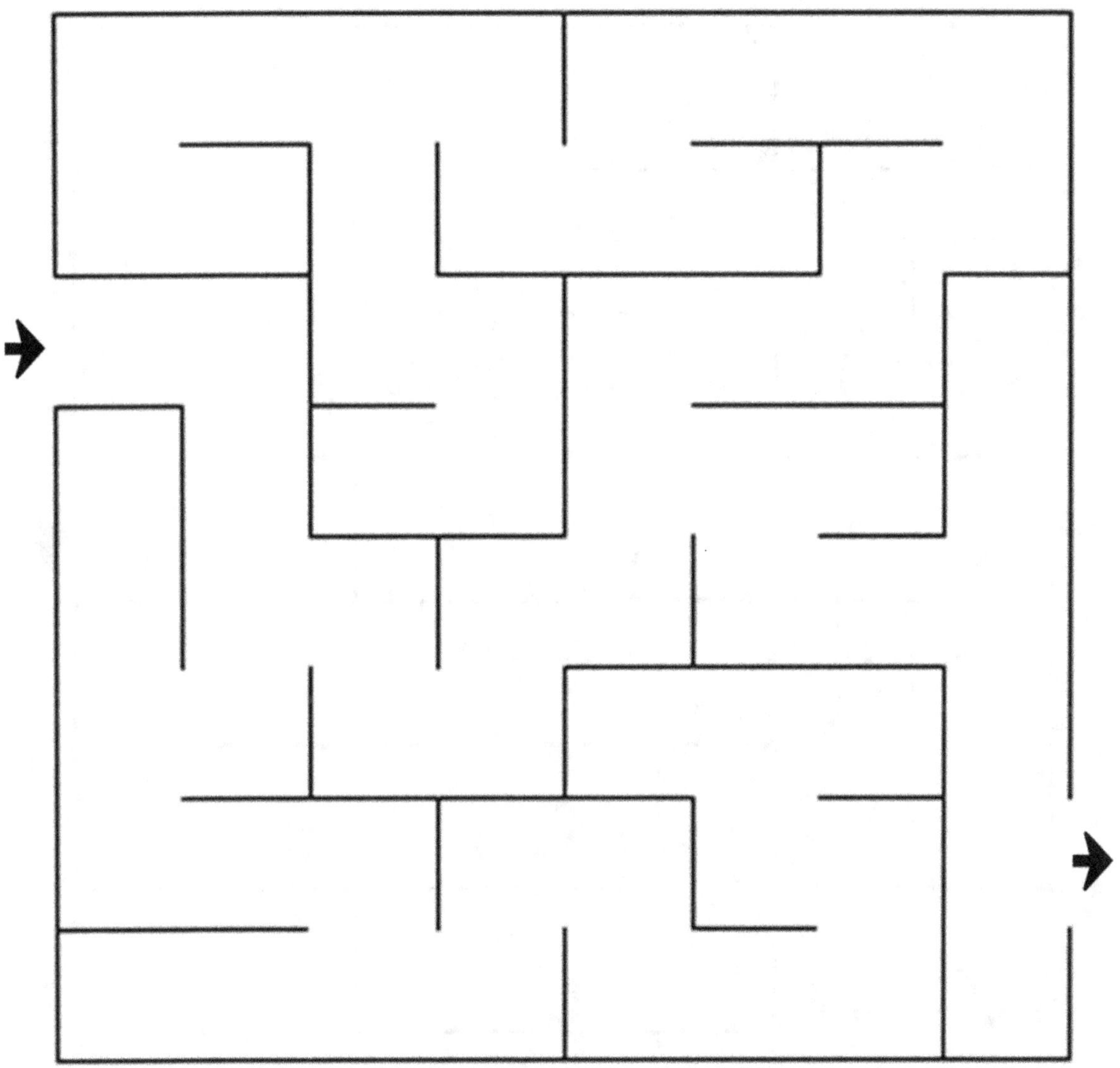

Name: _______________________   Date: _______________

48. Medium - Difficult

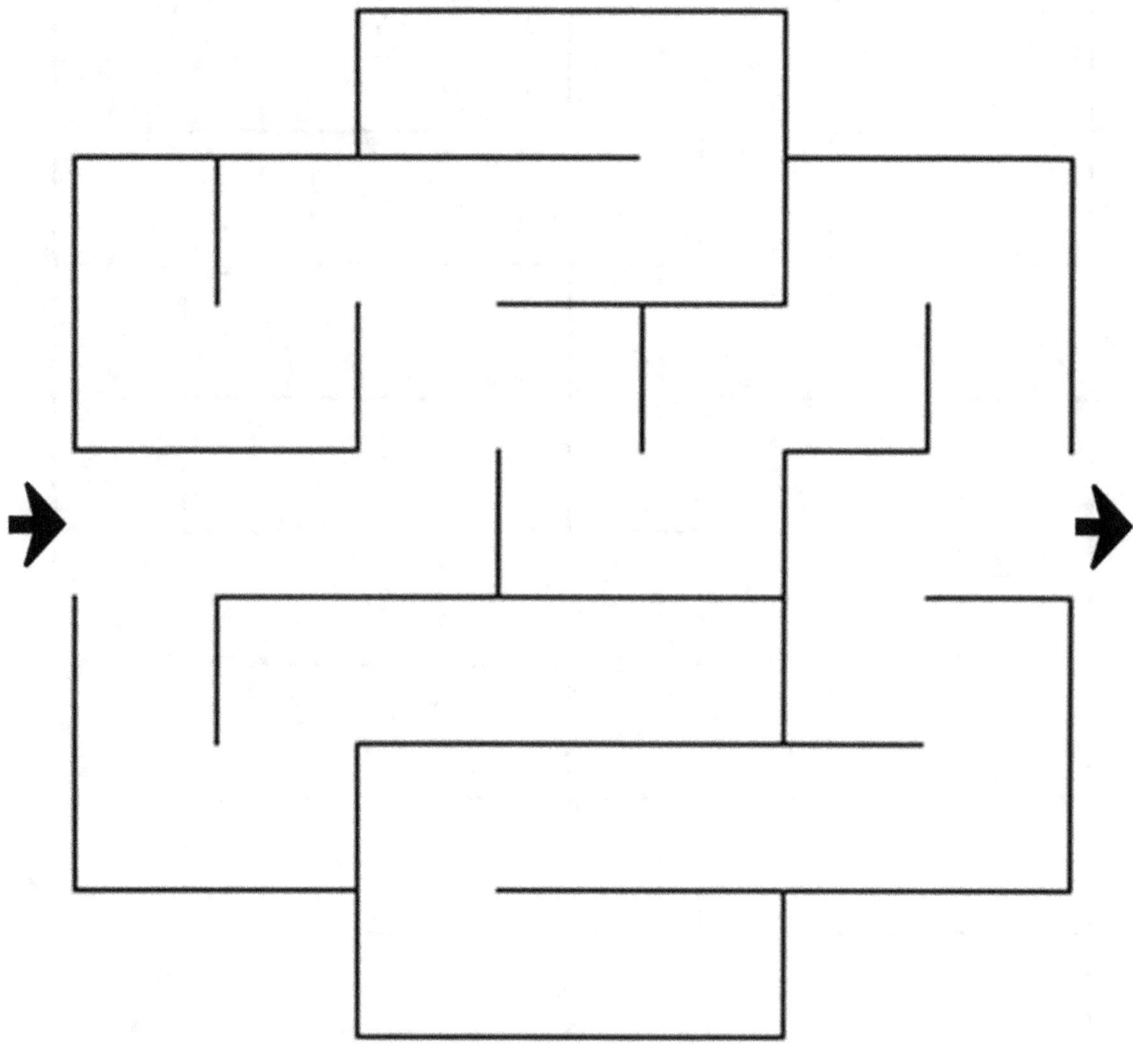

Name: ______________________   Date: ______________

49. Medium - Difficult

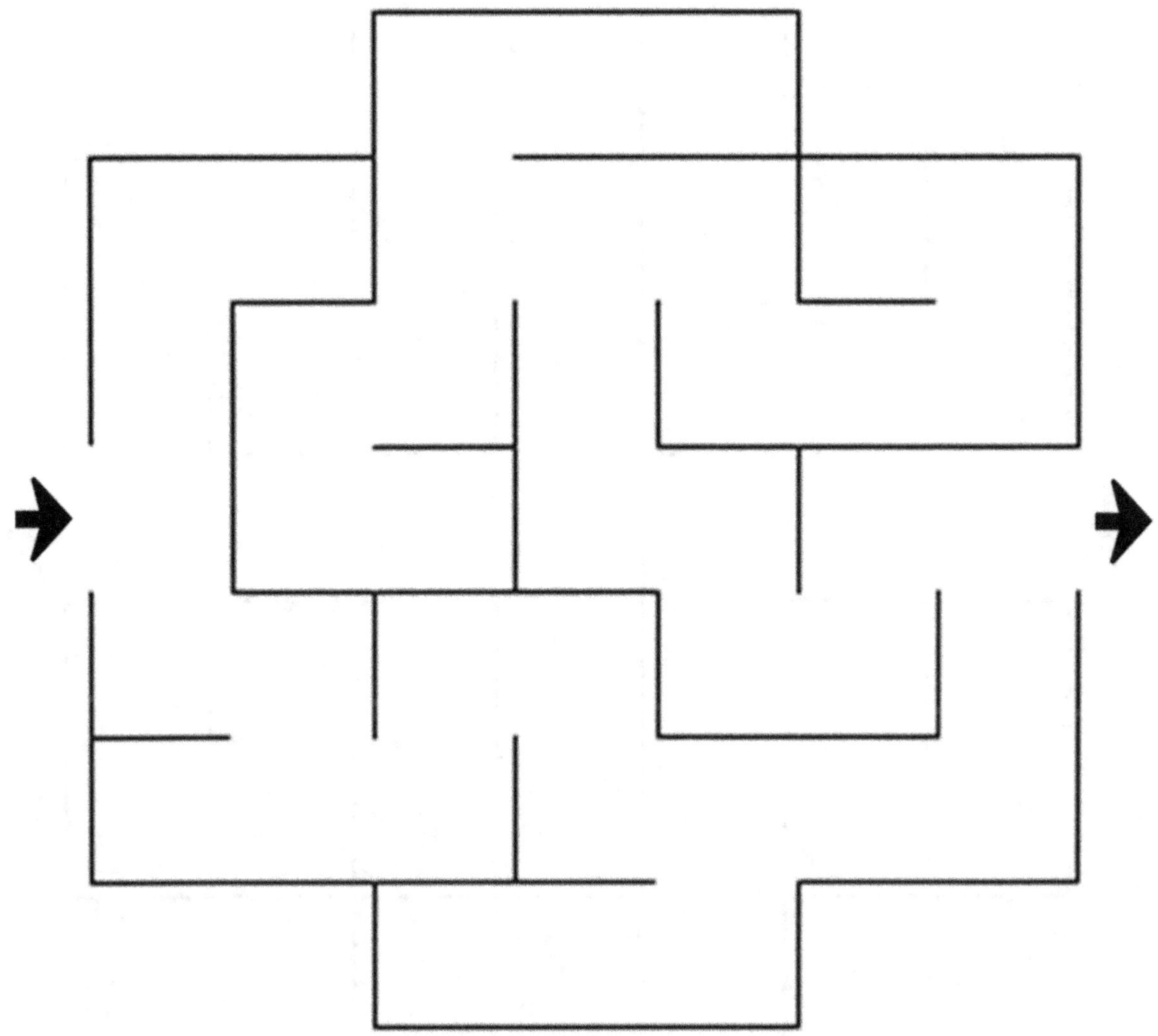

Name: _________________________   Date: _______________

50. Medium - Difficult

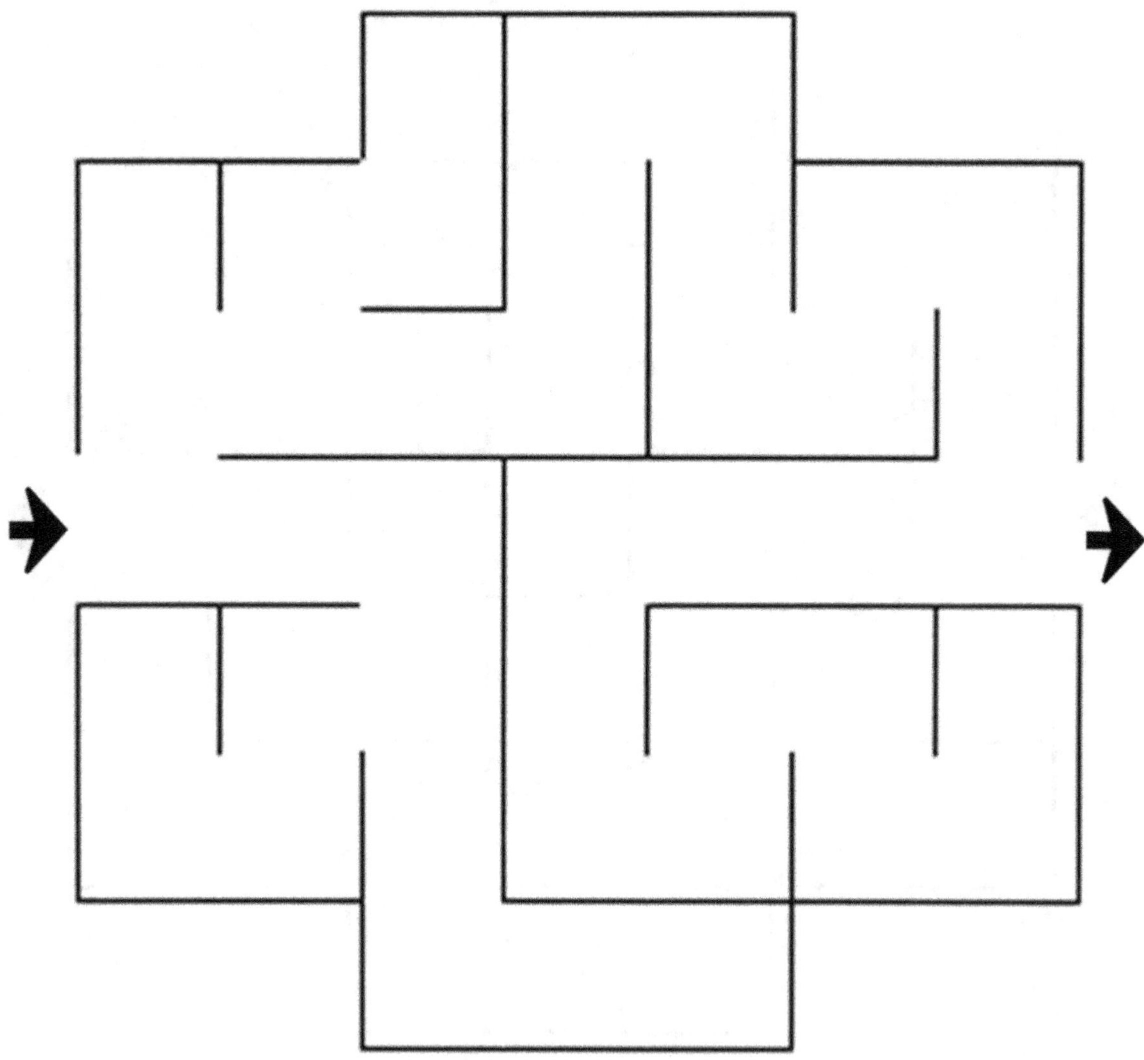

Name: __________________   Date: _____________

51. Medium - Difficult

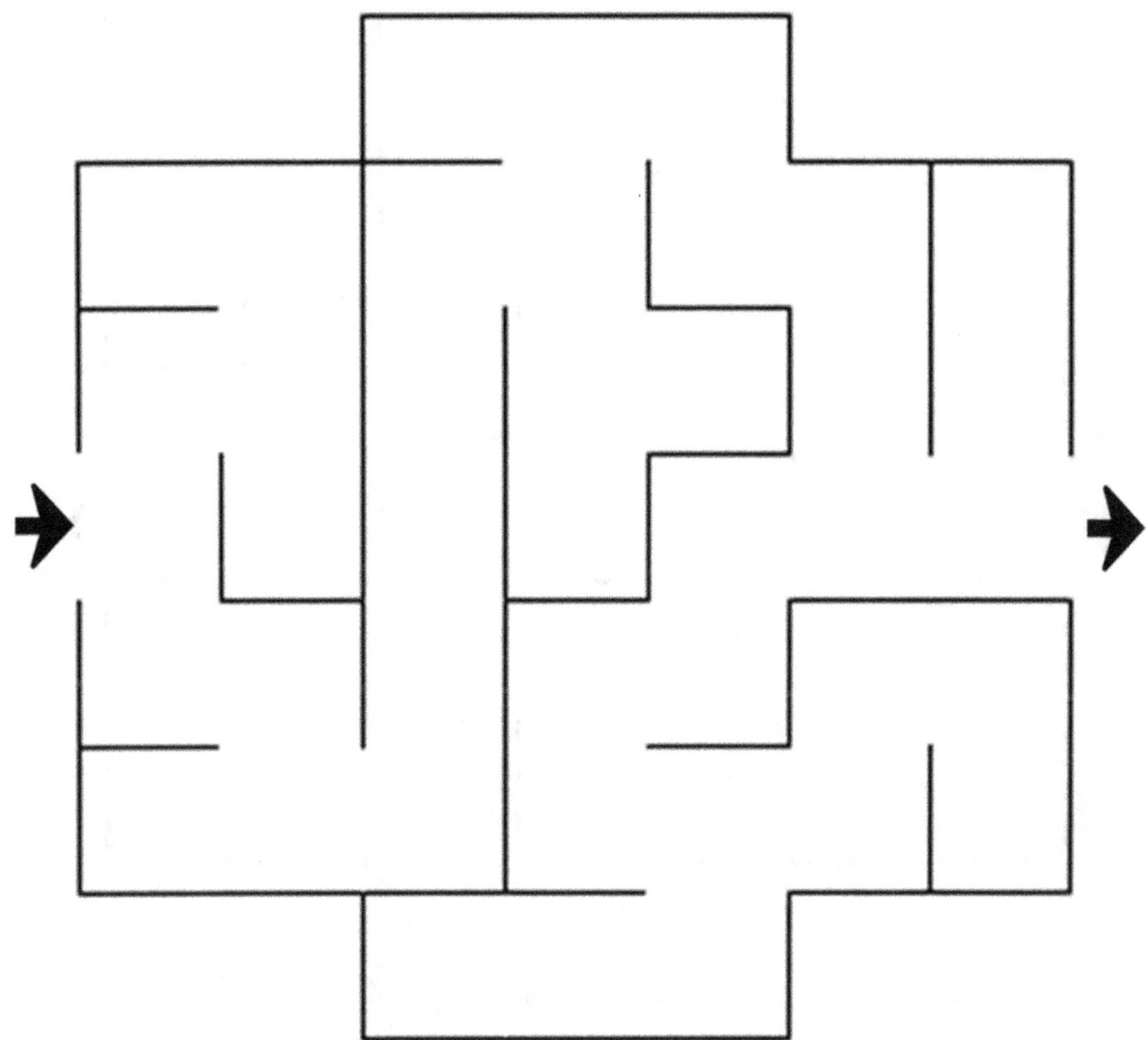

Name: _________________________   Date: _____________

52. Medium - Difficult

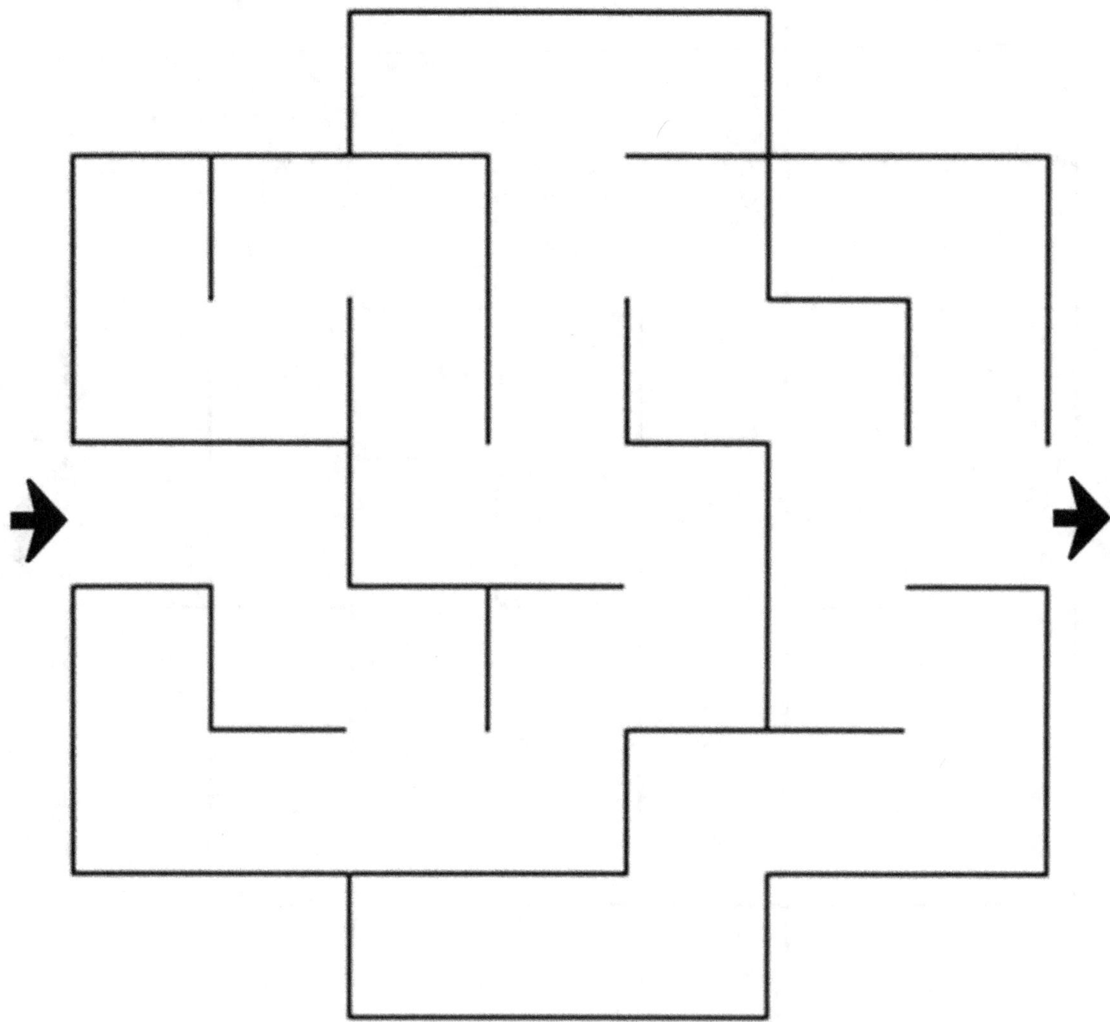

Name: ___________________   Date: _____________

53. Medium - Difficult

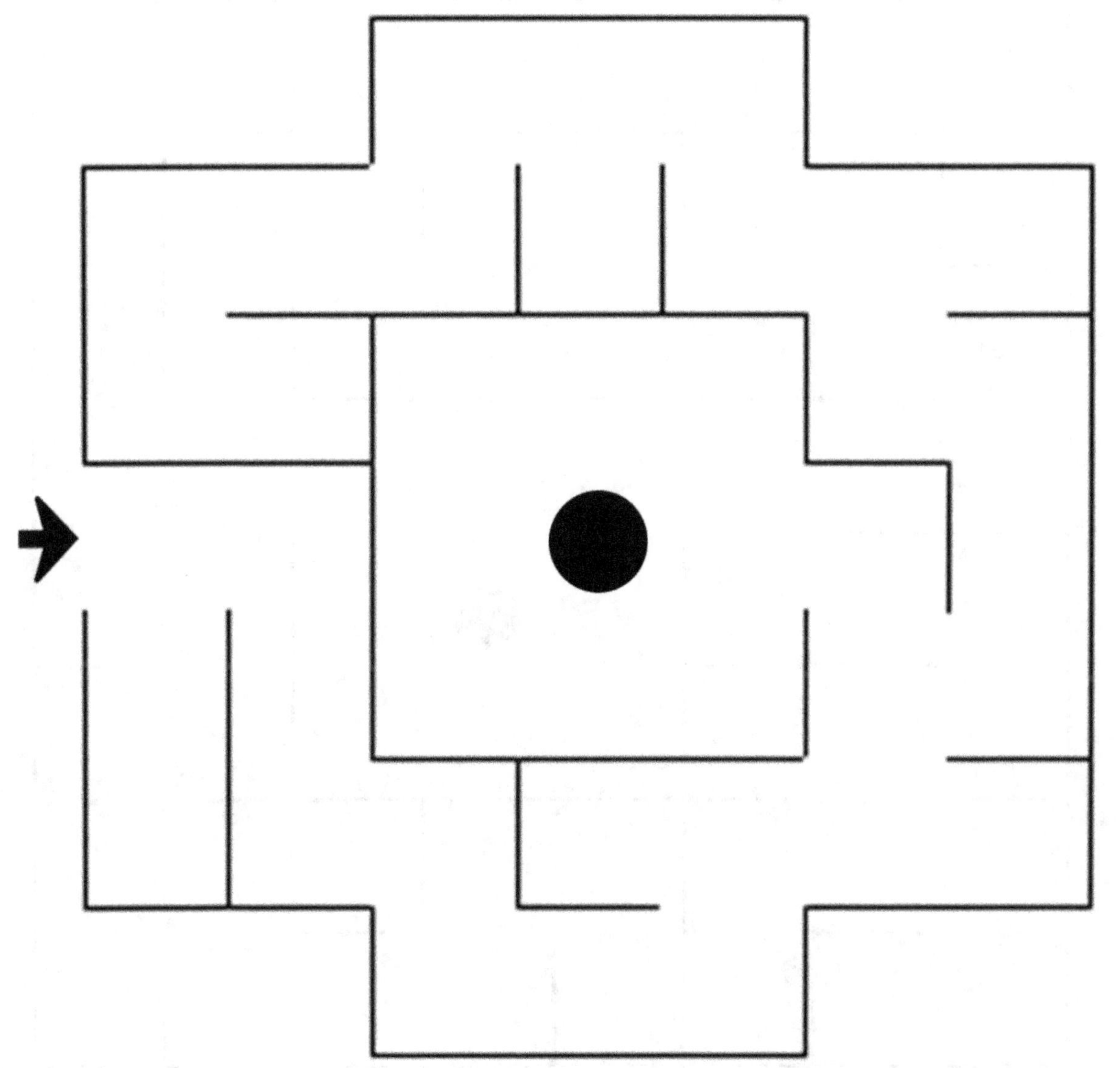

Name: _____________________   Date: _____________

54. Medium - Difficult

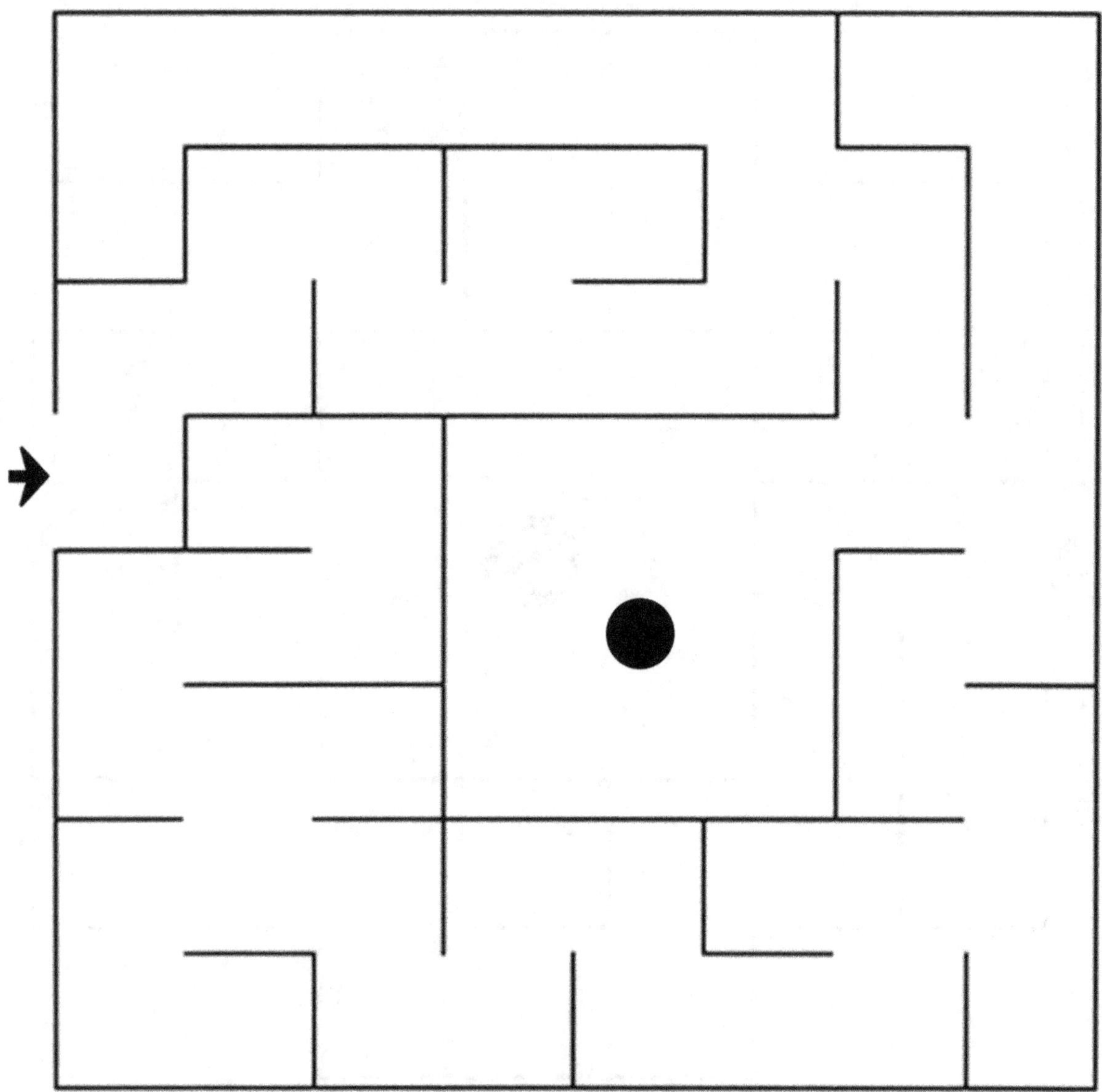

Name: _______________________   Date: _______________

55. Difficult

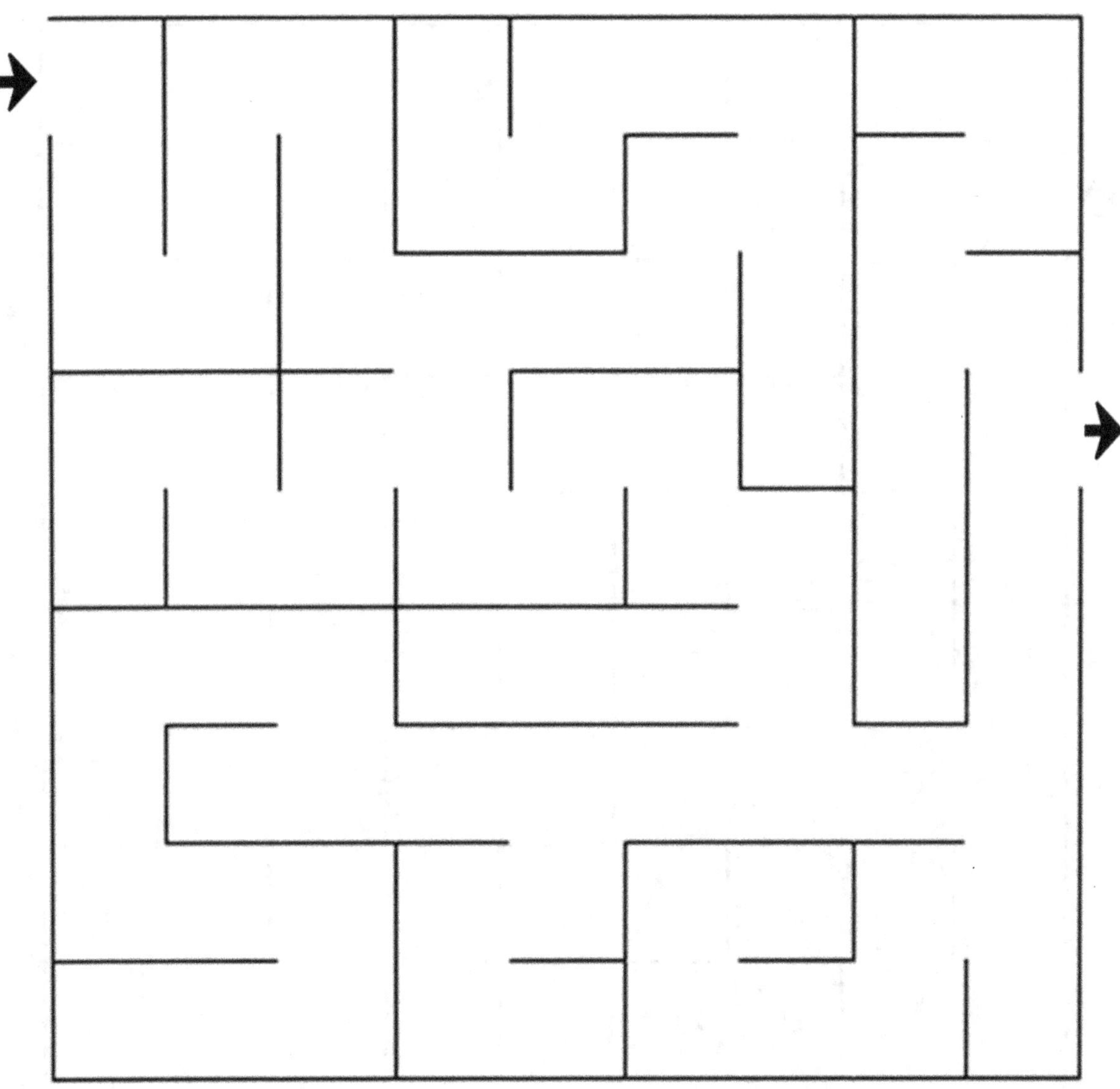

Name: _____________________   Date: _____________

56. Difficult

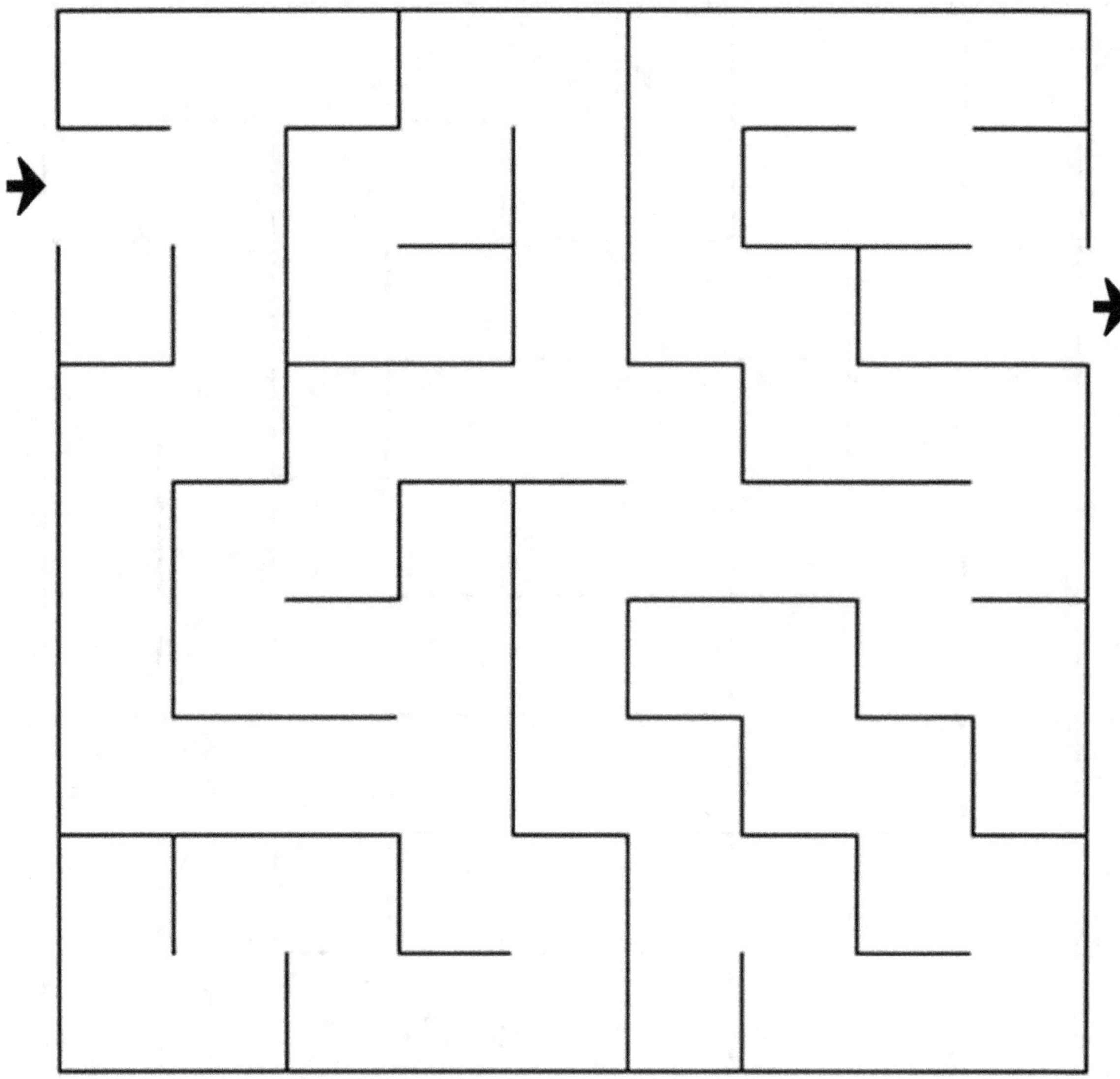

Name: _______________________   Date: _______________

57. Difficult

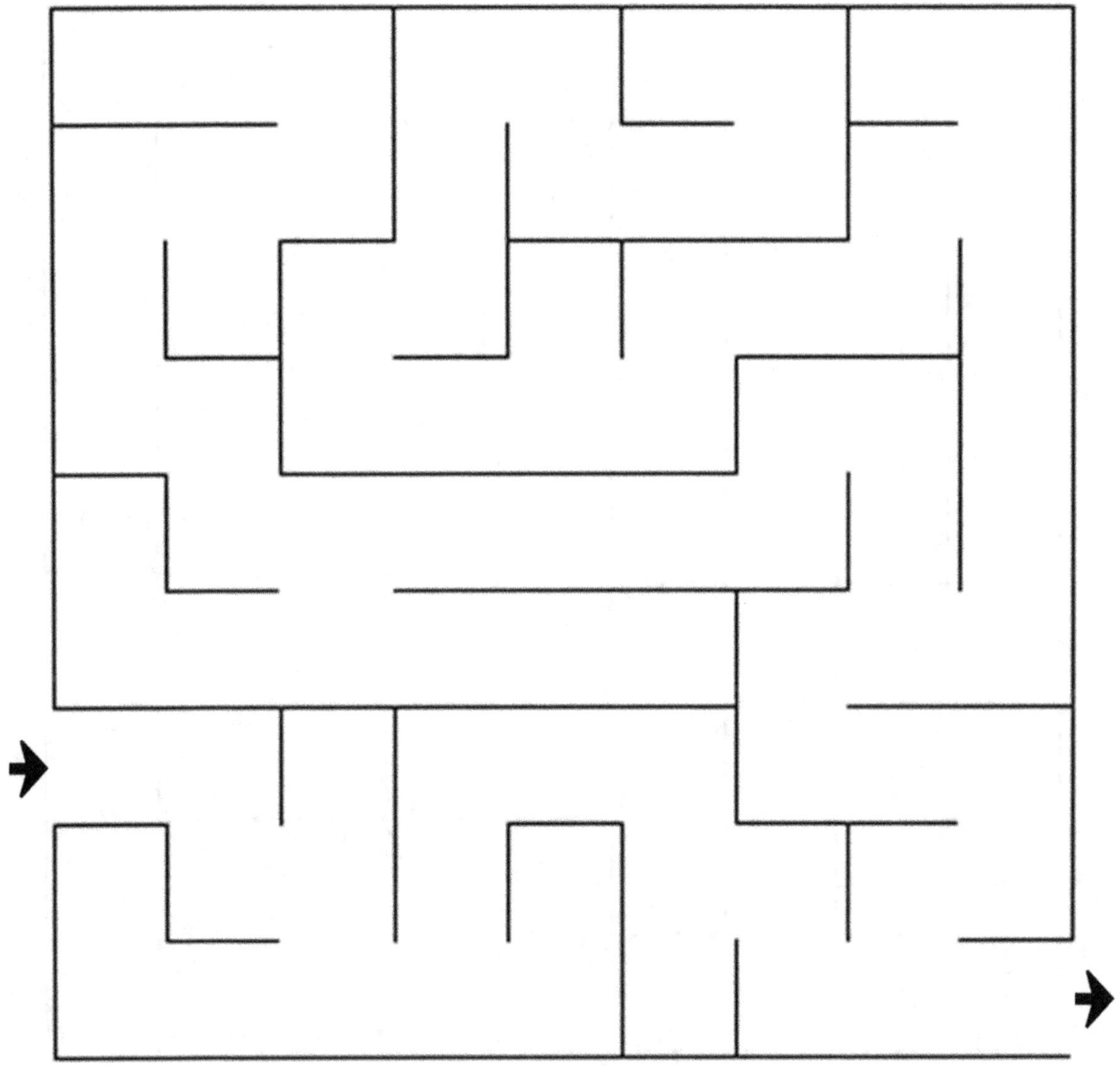

Name: _______________________

Date: _______________

58. Difficult

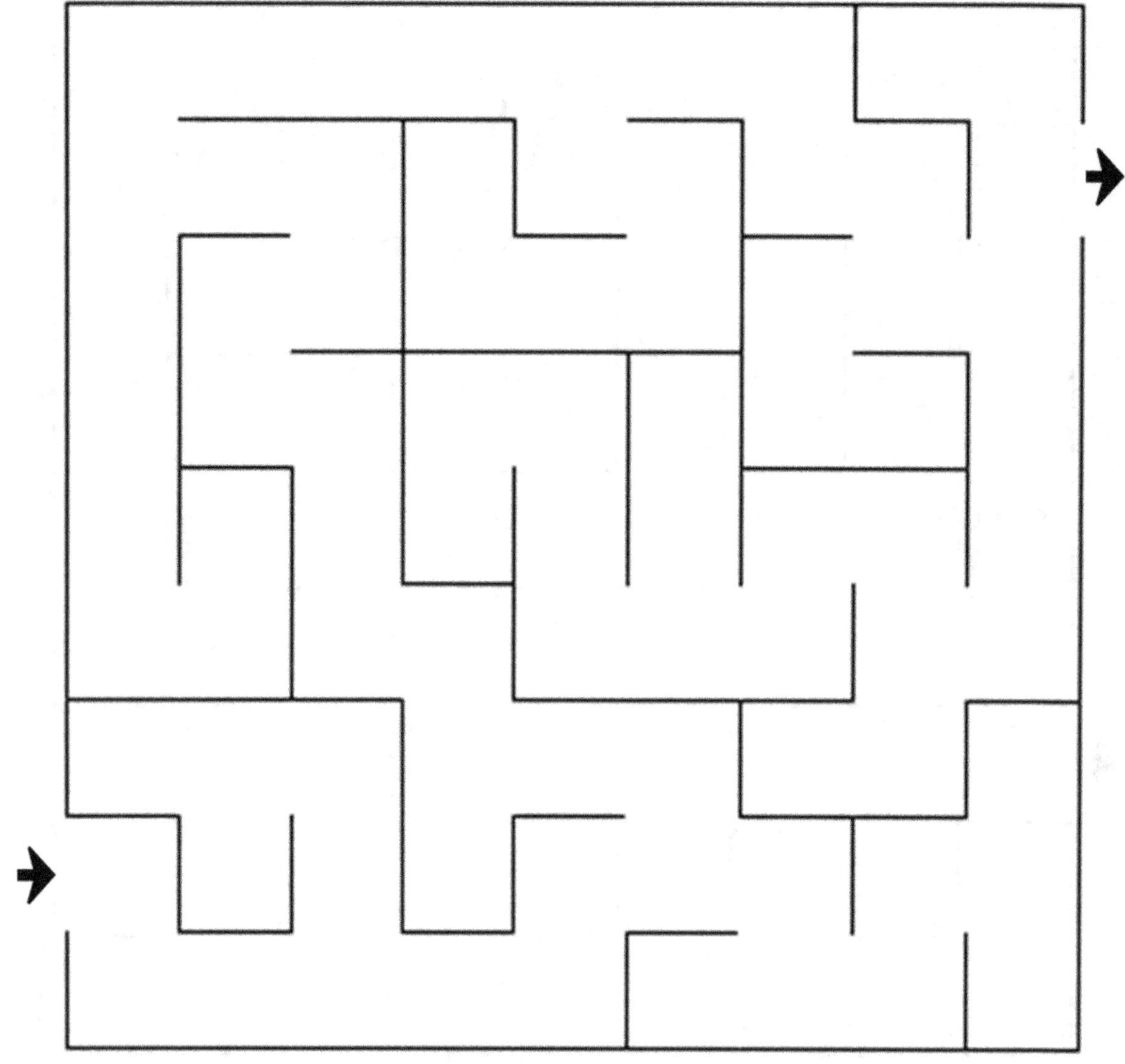

Name: ______________________   Date: ______________

59. Difficult

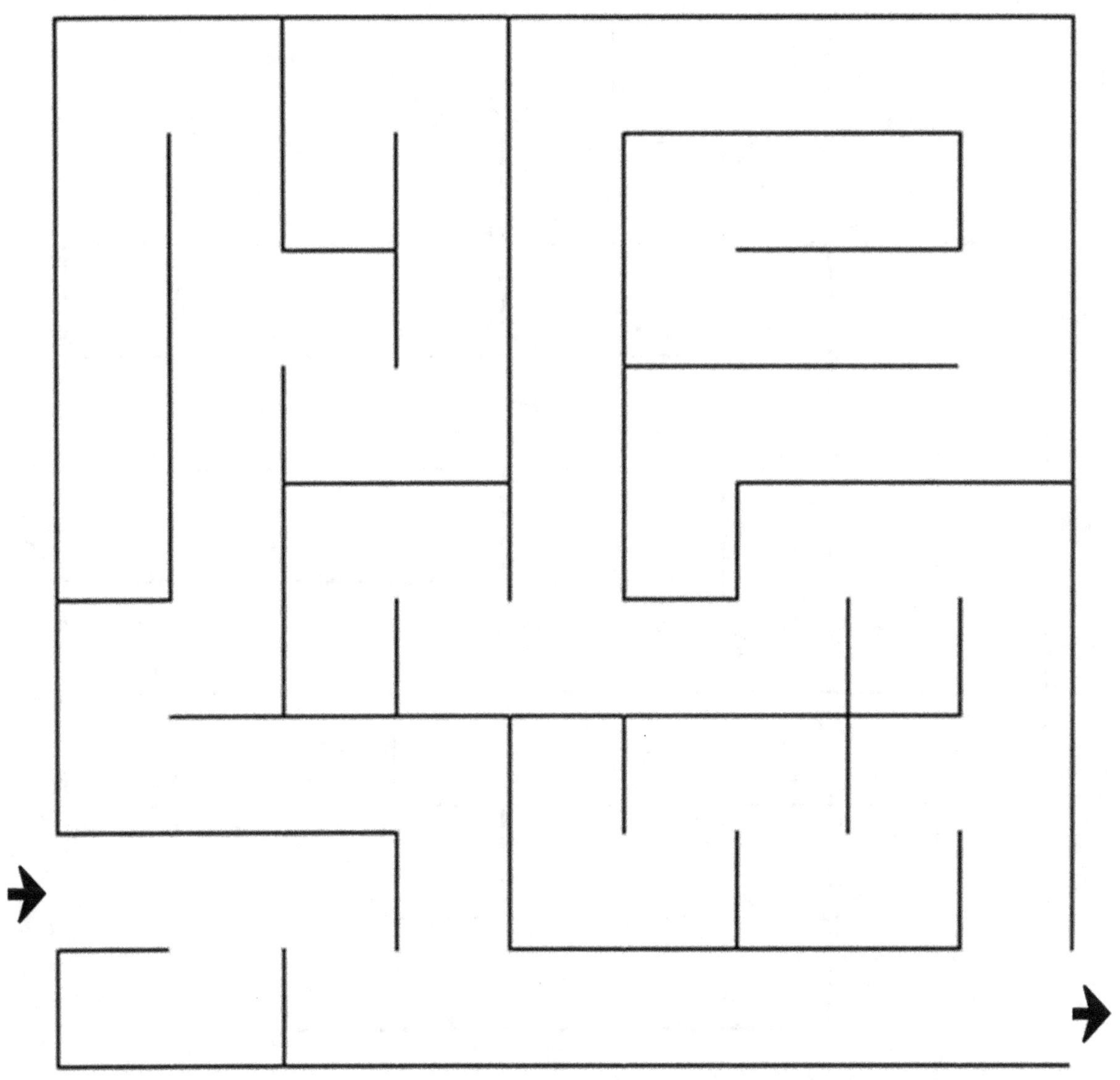

Name: _______________________   Date: _______________

60. Difficult

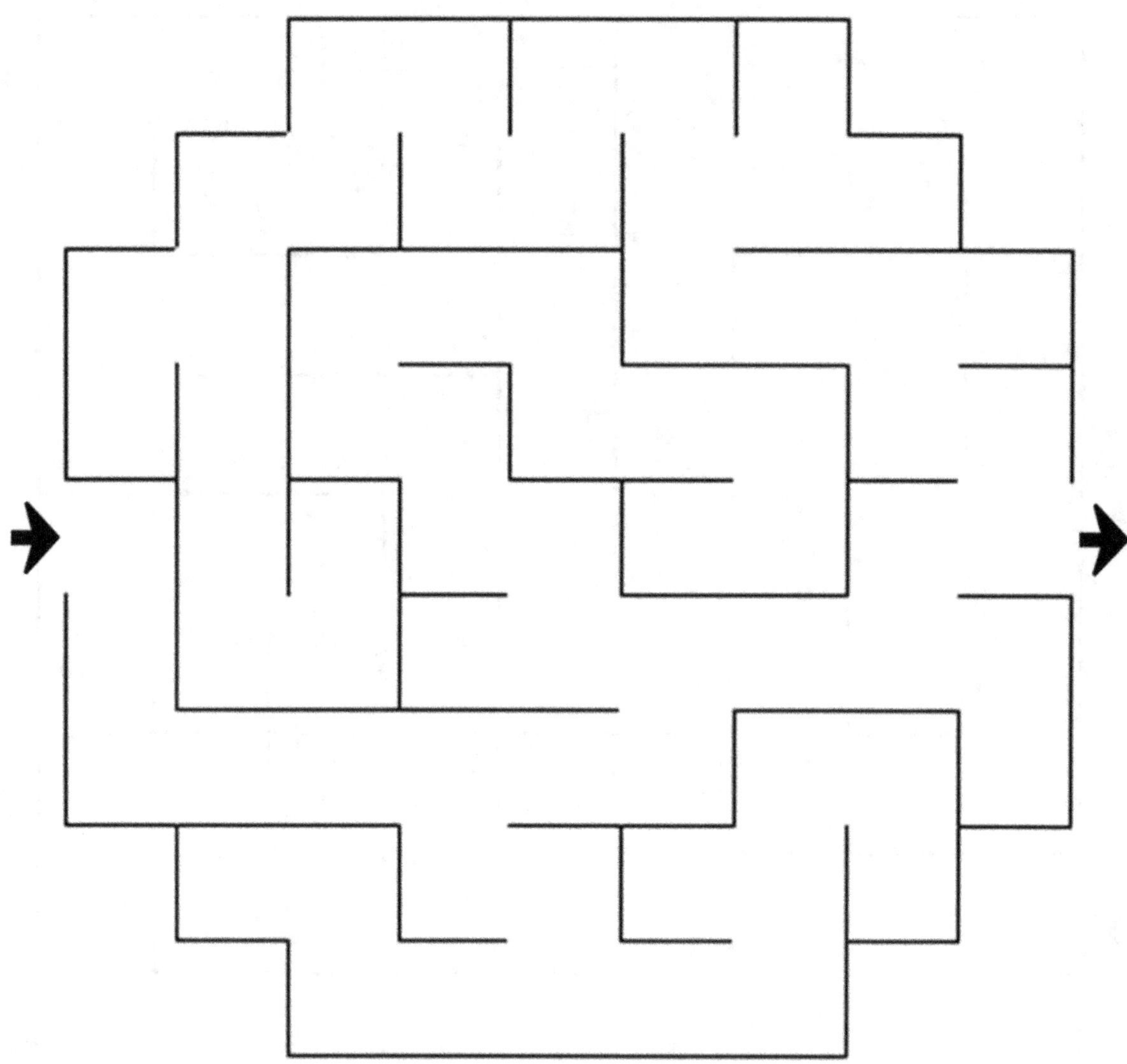

Name: ___________________   Date: _____________

61. Difficult

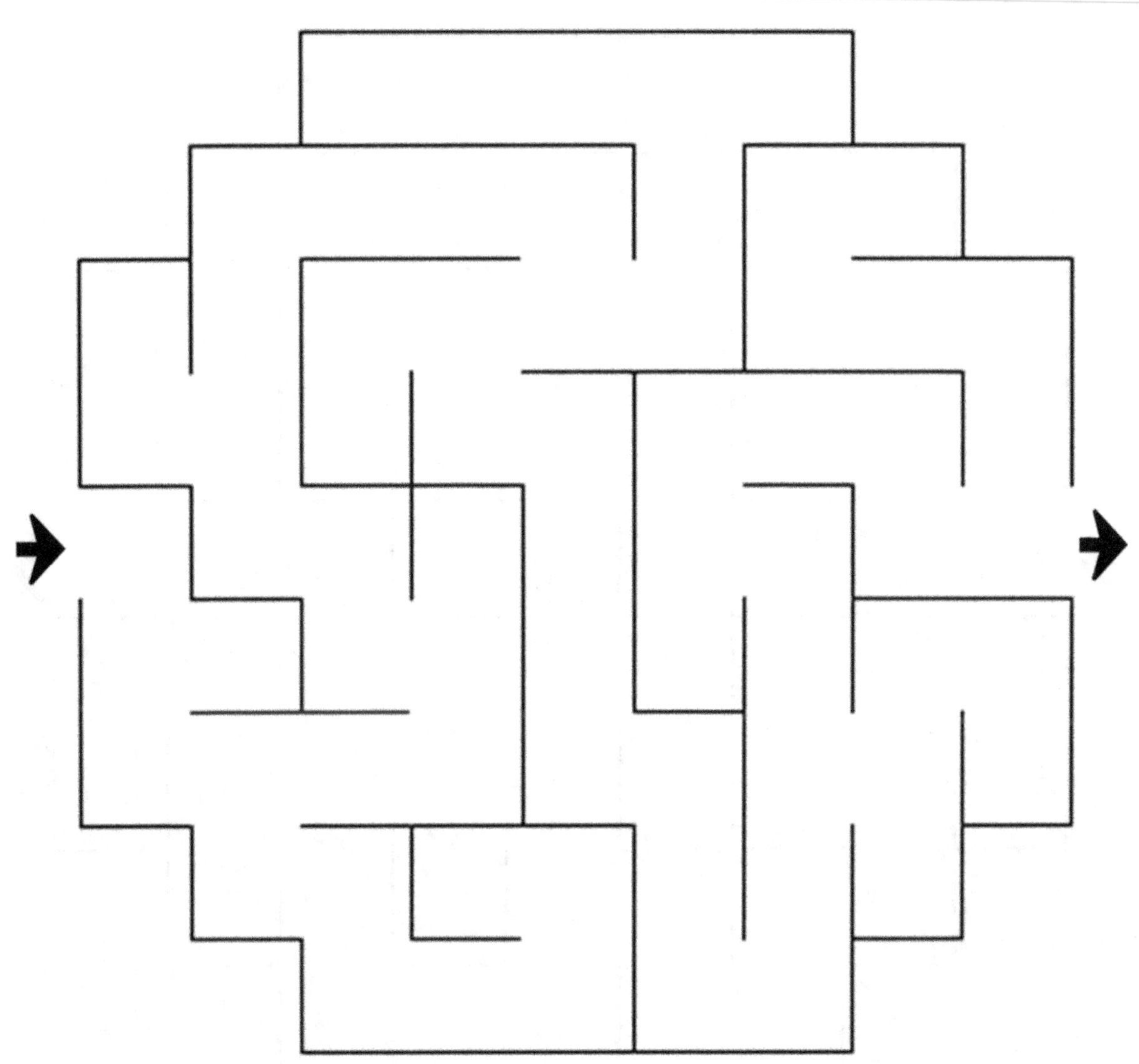

Name: _____________________   Date: _____________

62. Difficult

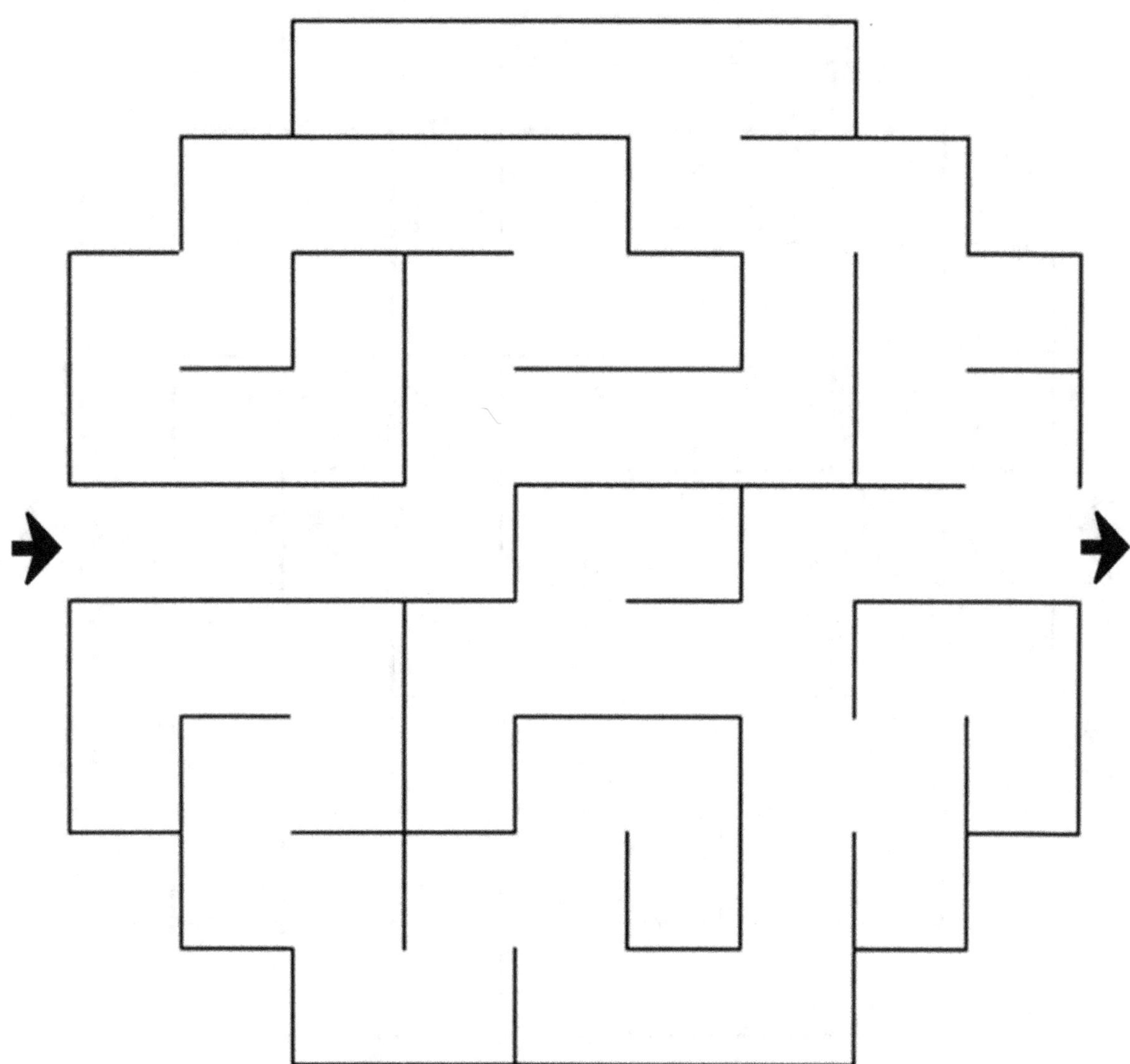

Kindergarten Mazes

Name: _____________________   Date: _____________

63. Difficult

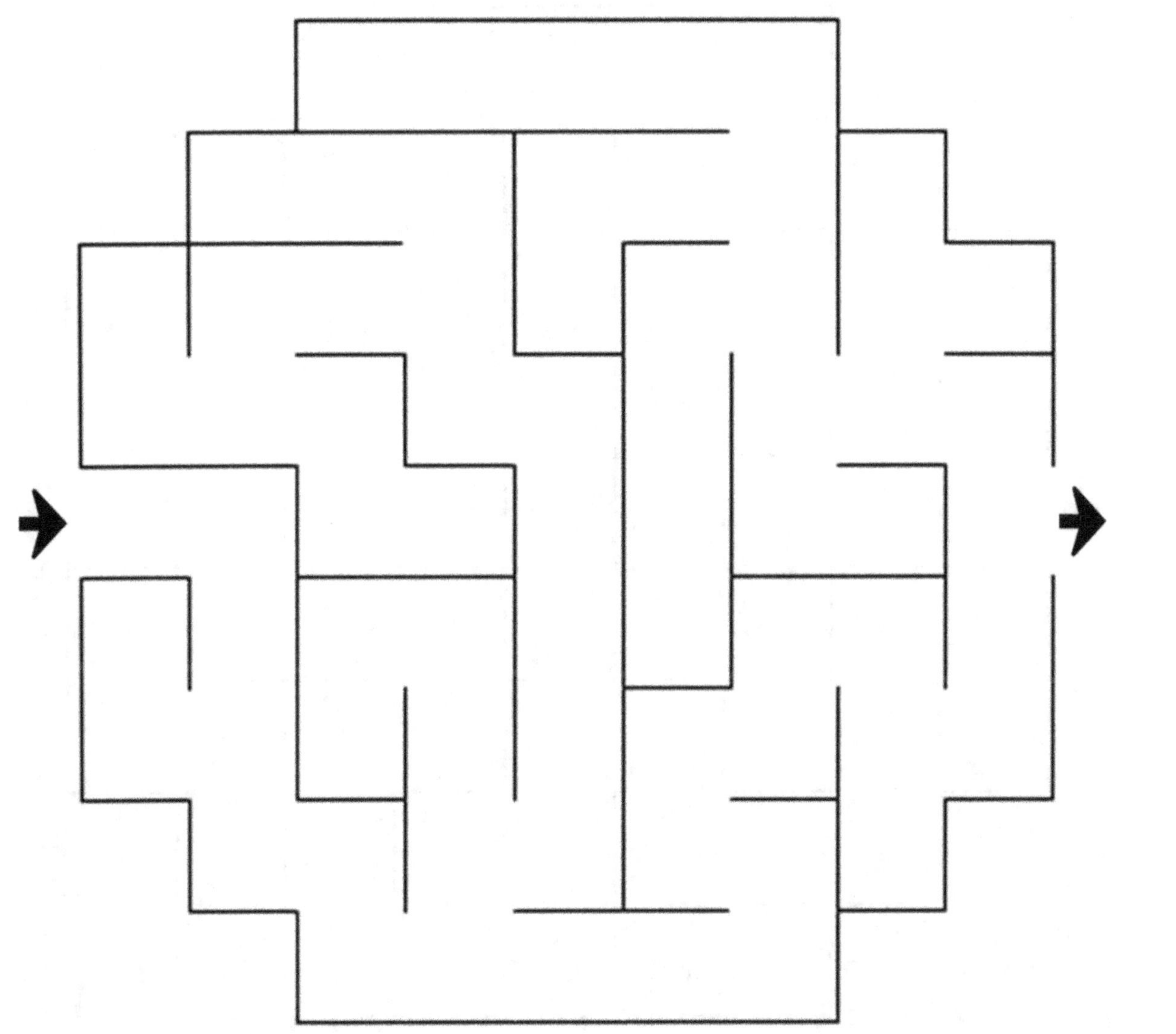

Name: ______________________   Date: ____________

64. Difficult

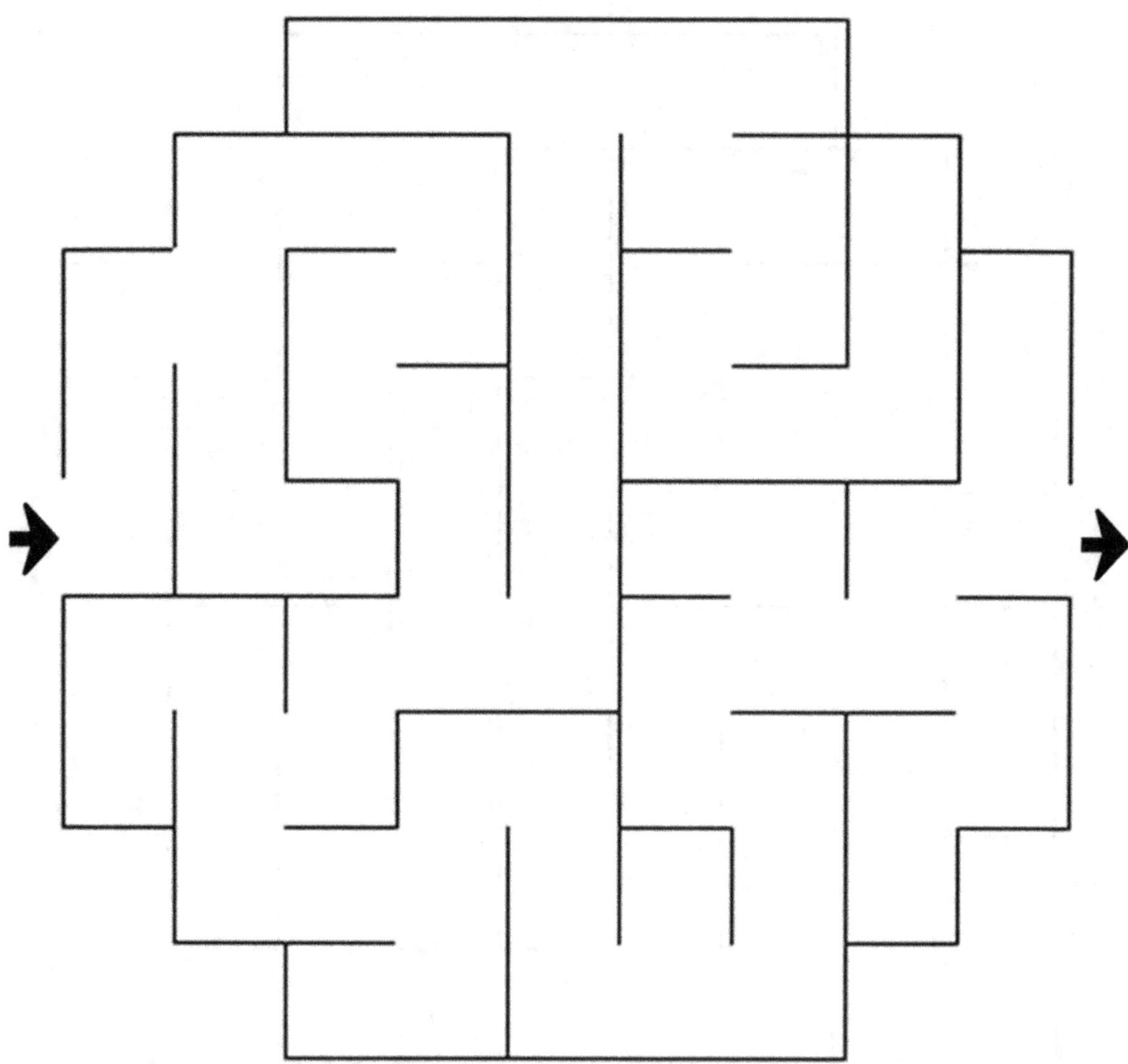

Name: ___________________   Date: ____________

65. Difficult

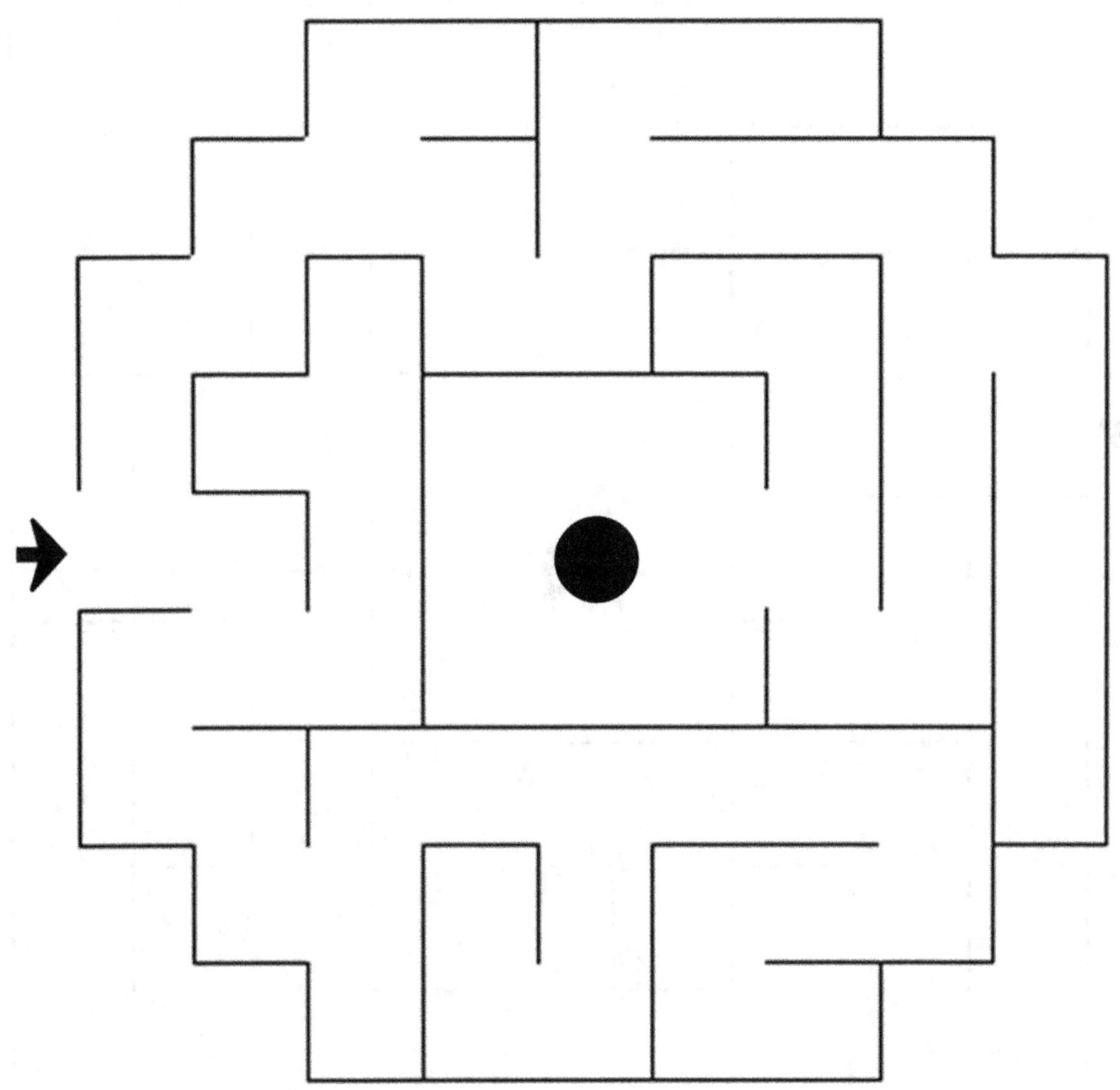

Name: _______________________   Date: _____________

66. Difficult

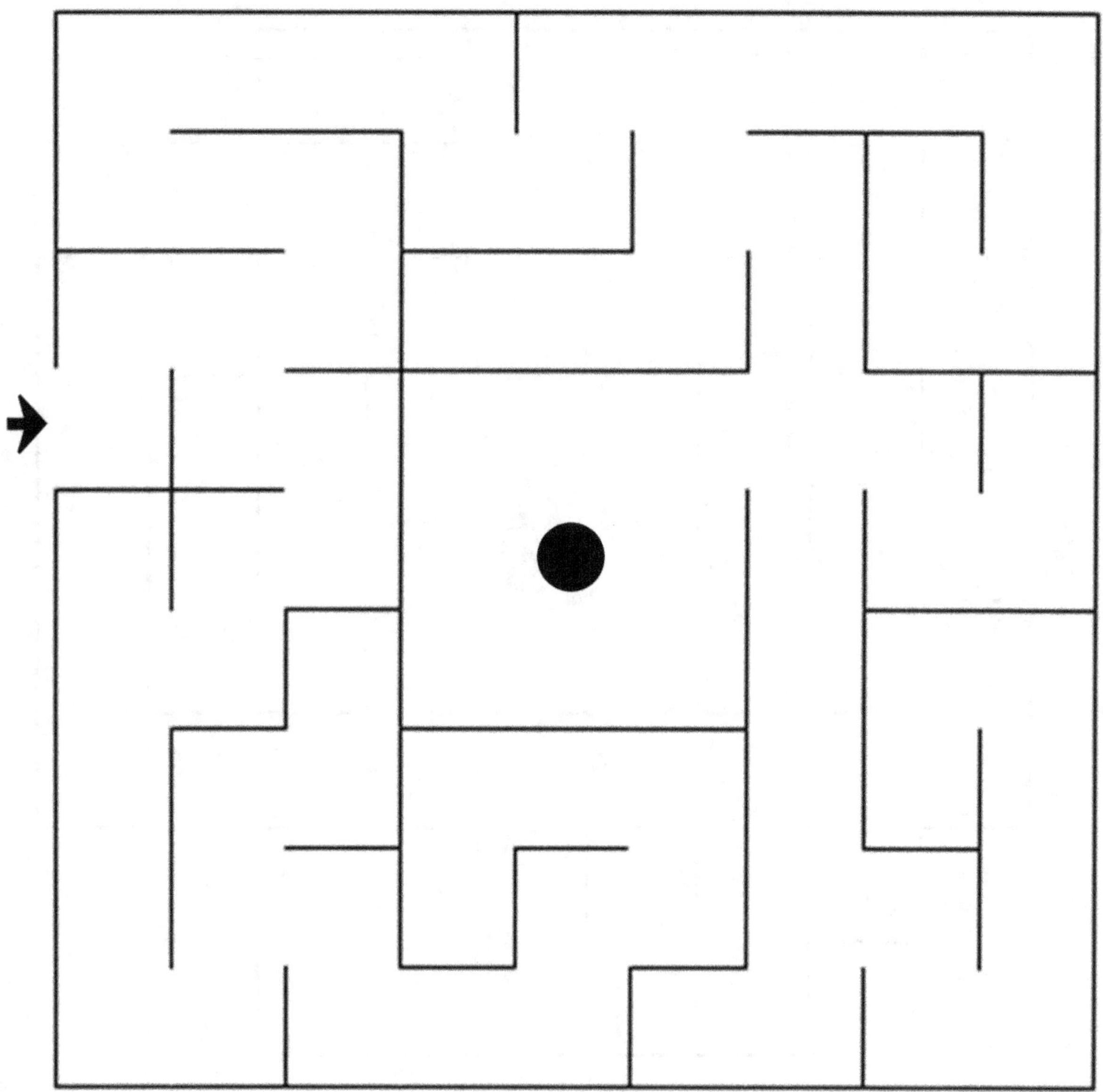

Kindergarten Mazes

Name: ______________________   Date: ______________

67. Super - Difficult

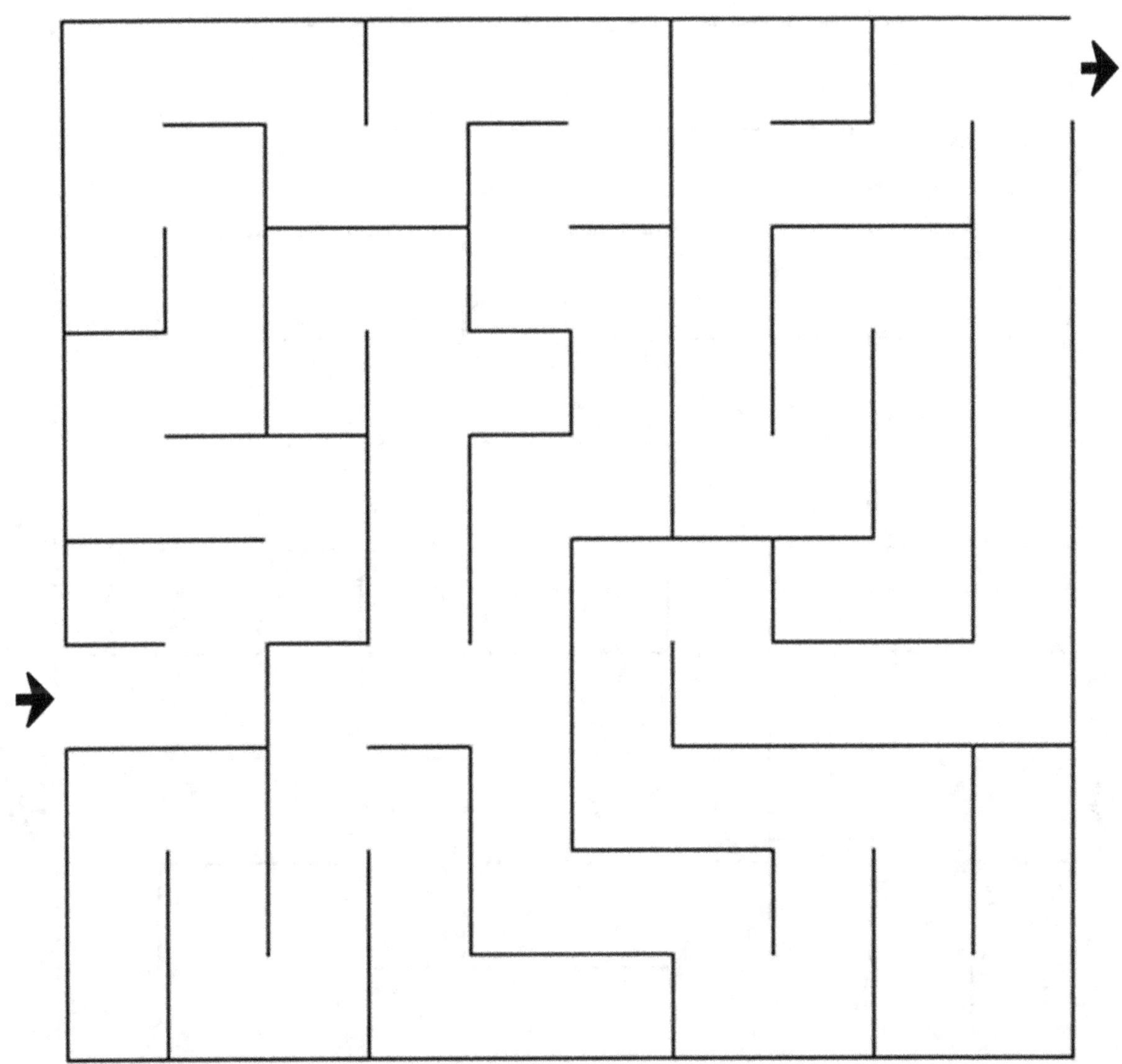

Name: _________________________   Date: _____________

68. Super - Difficult

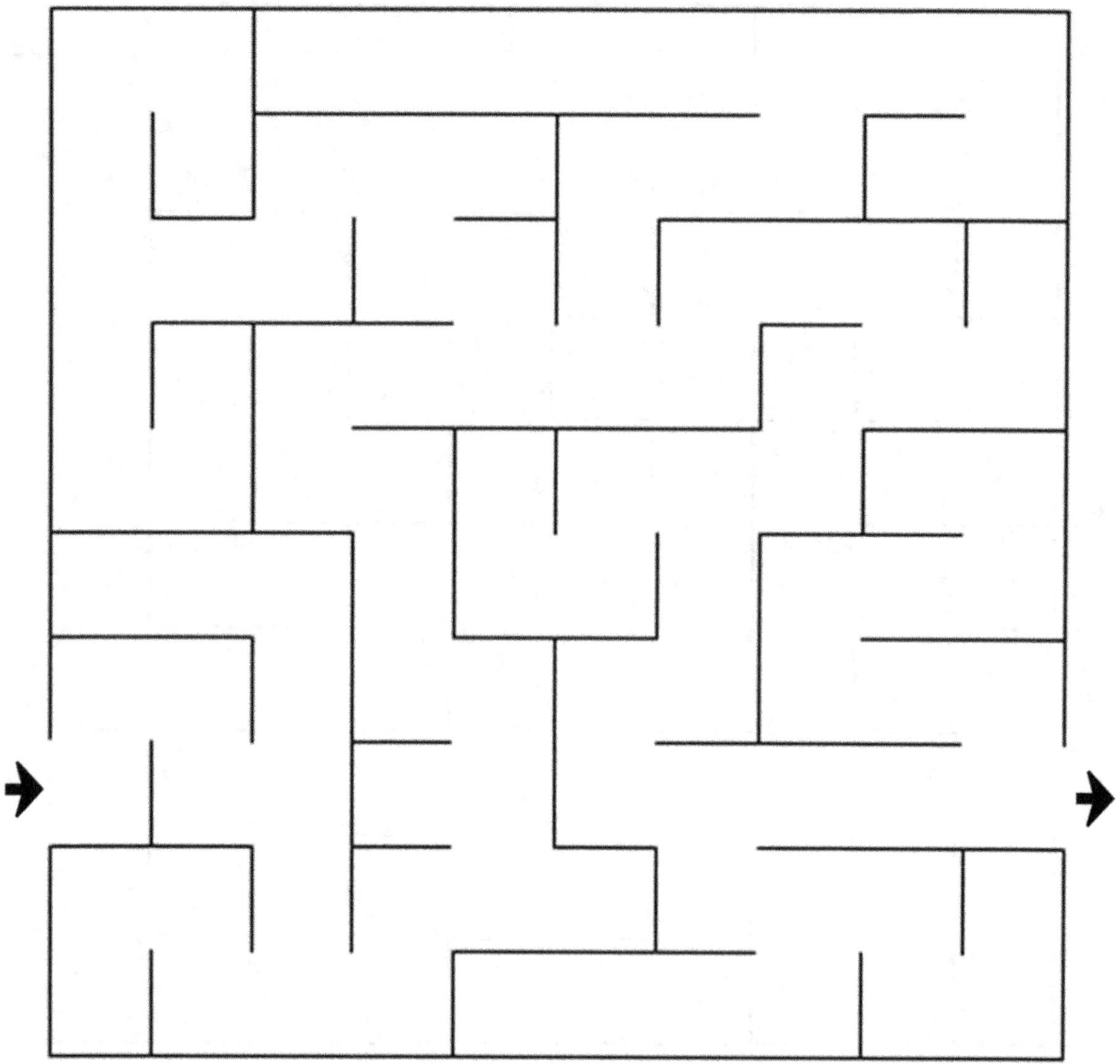

Name: _______________________   Date: _____________

69. Super - Difficult

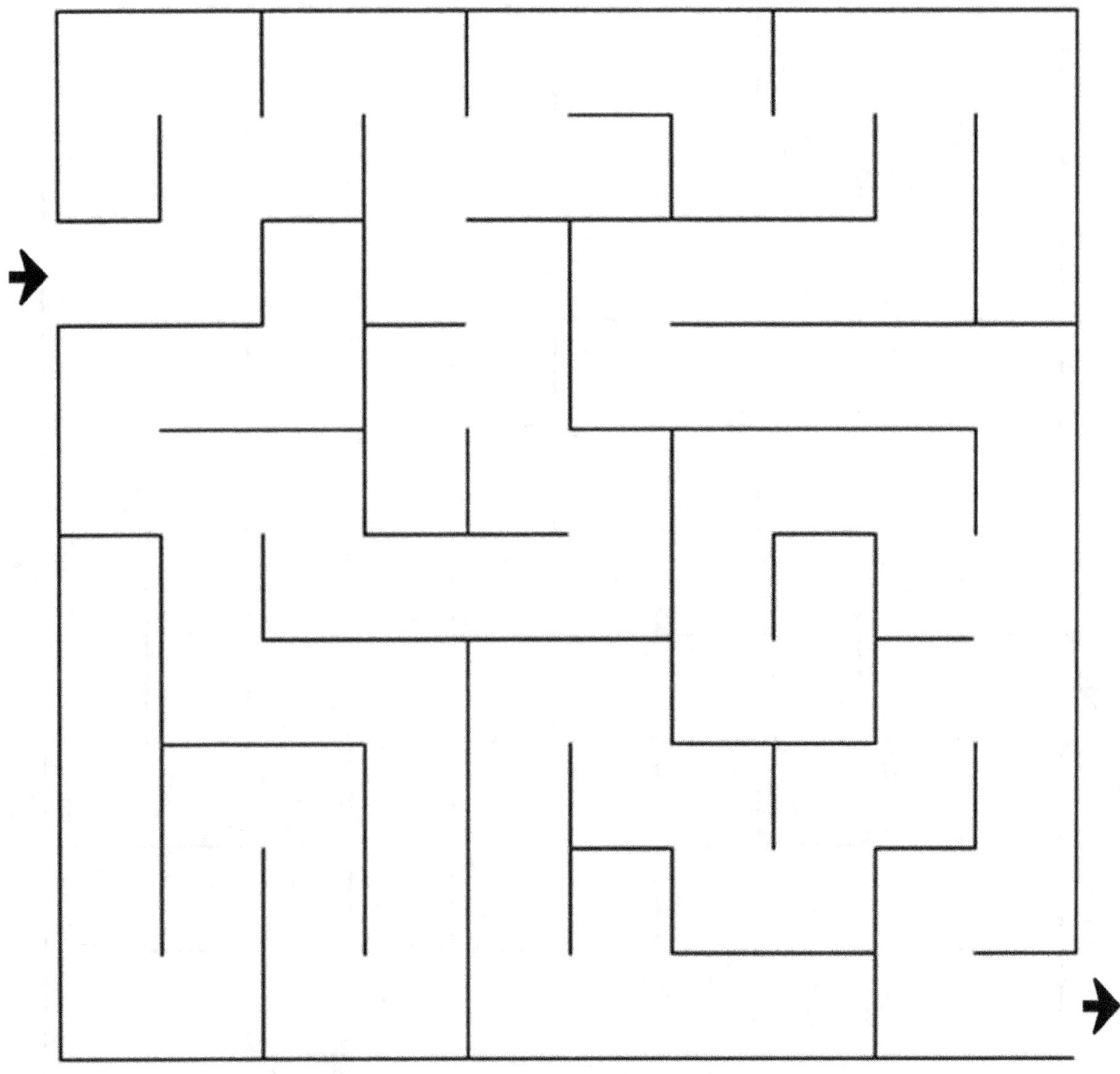

Name: _________________   Date: _____________

70. Super - Difficult

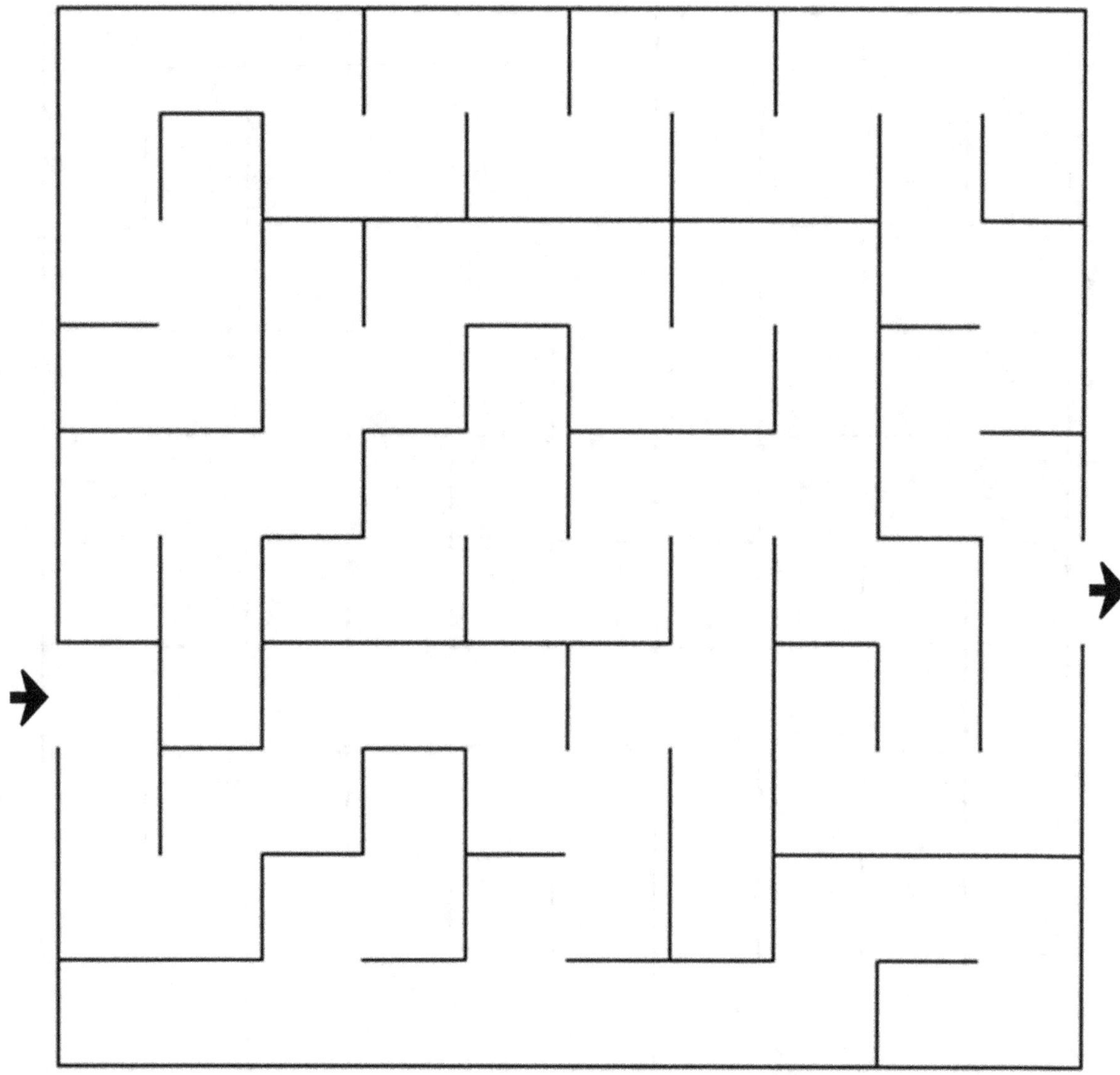

Kindergarten Mazes

Name: ___________________   Date: _____________

71. Super - Difficult

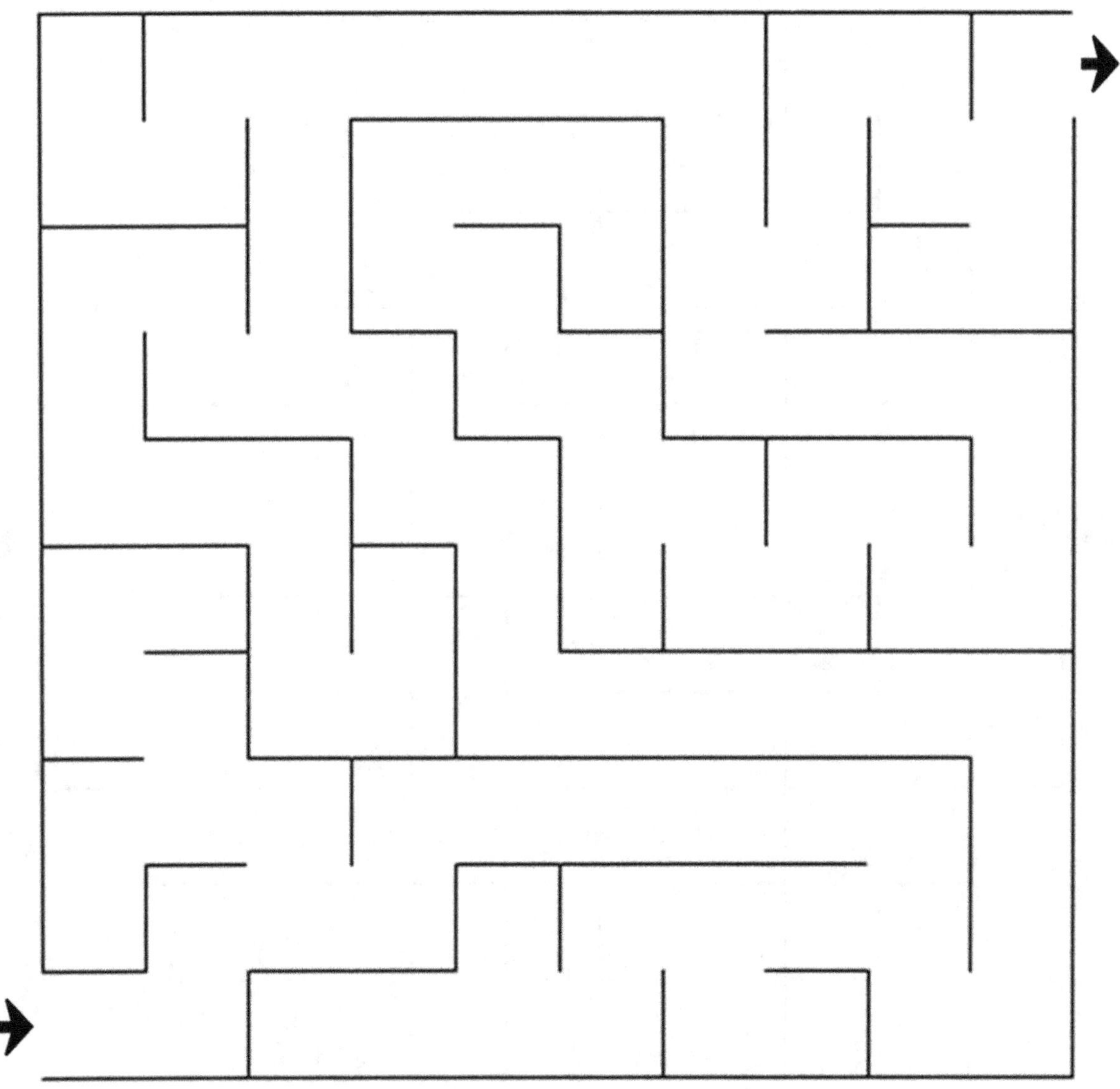

Name: _______________________

Date: _____________

72. Super - Difficult

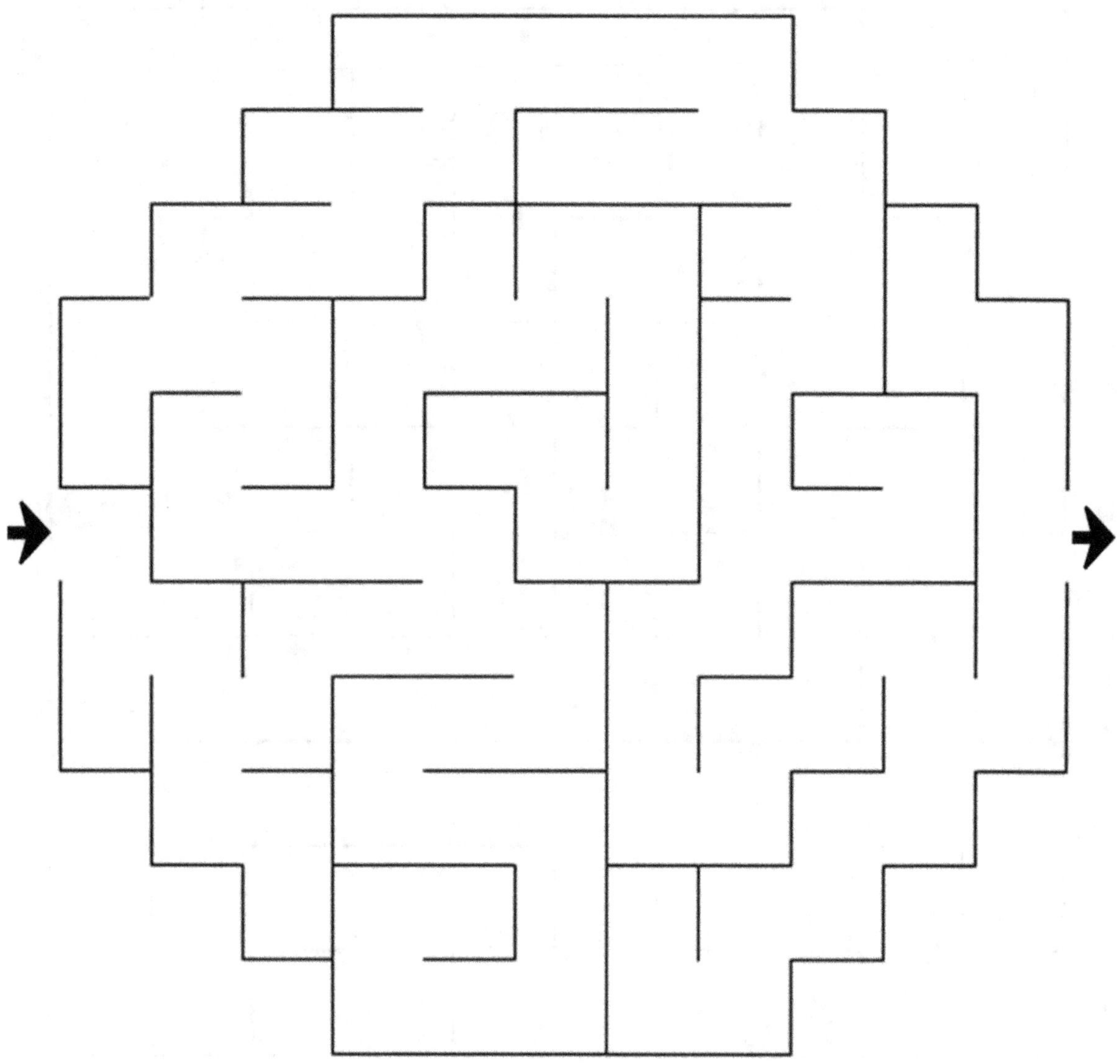

Name: _____________________   Date: ____________

73. Super - Difficult

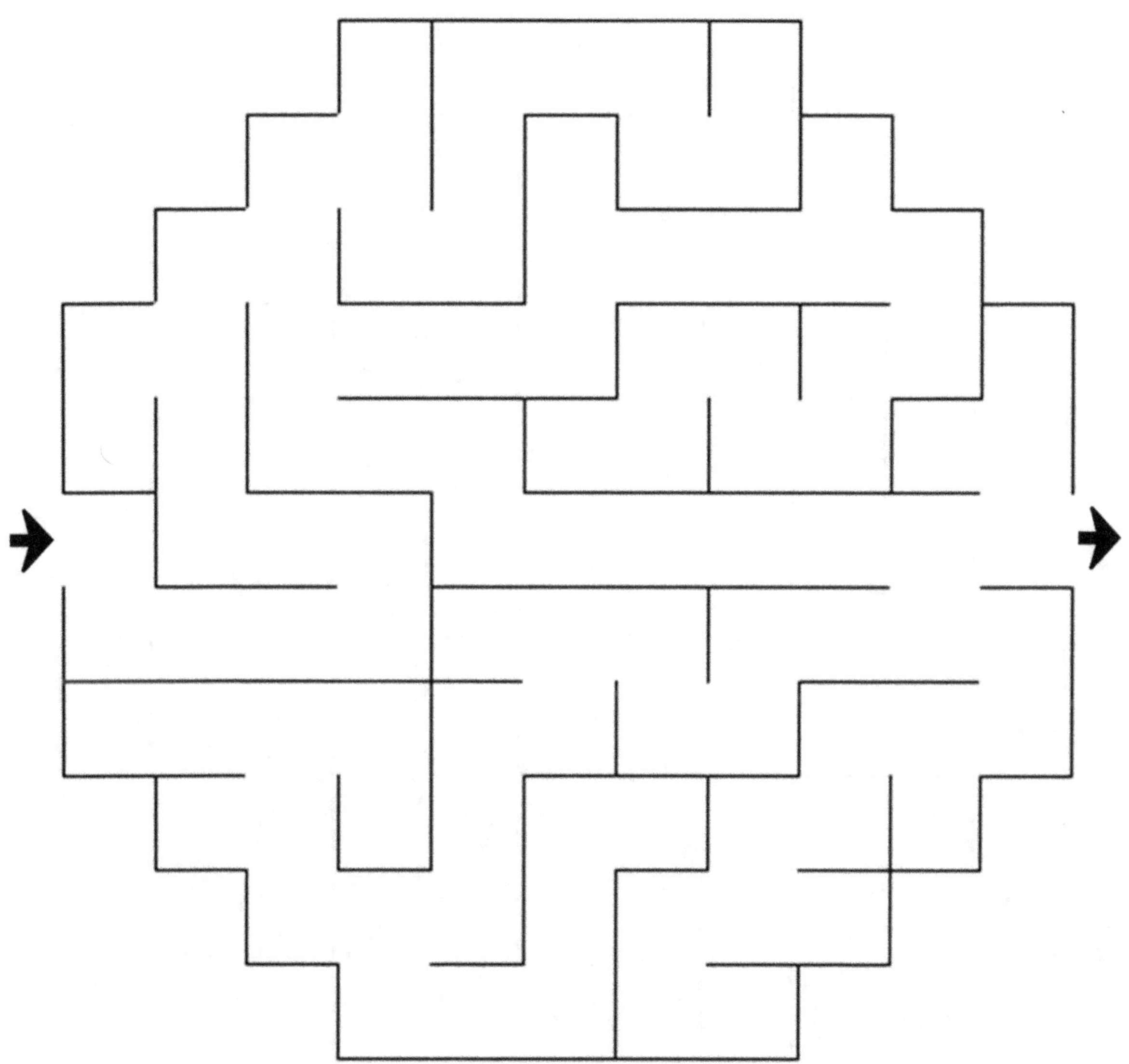

Name: _________________________ Date: ______________

74. Super - Difficult

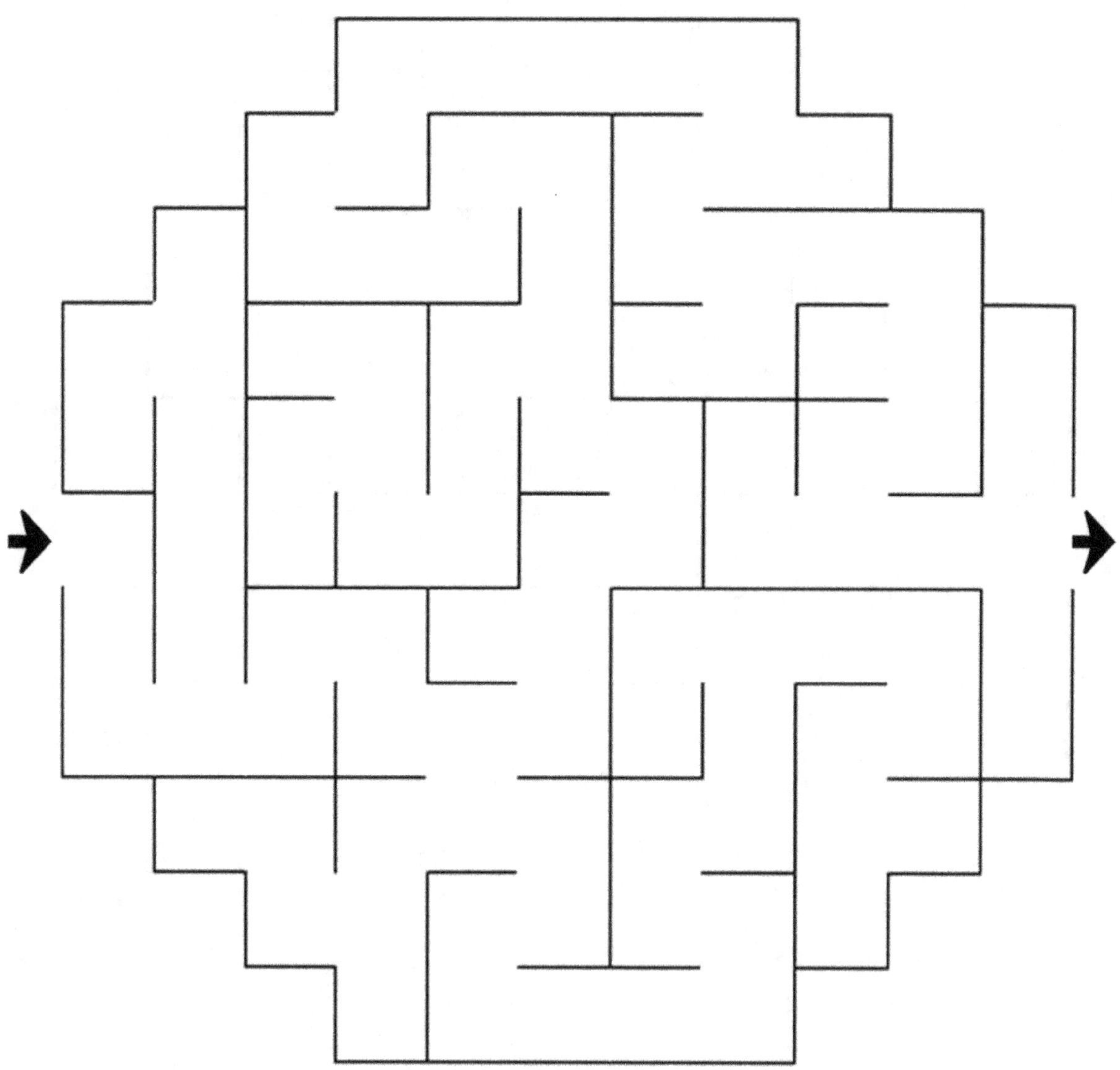

Name: ___________________   Date: _____________

75. Super - Difficult

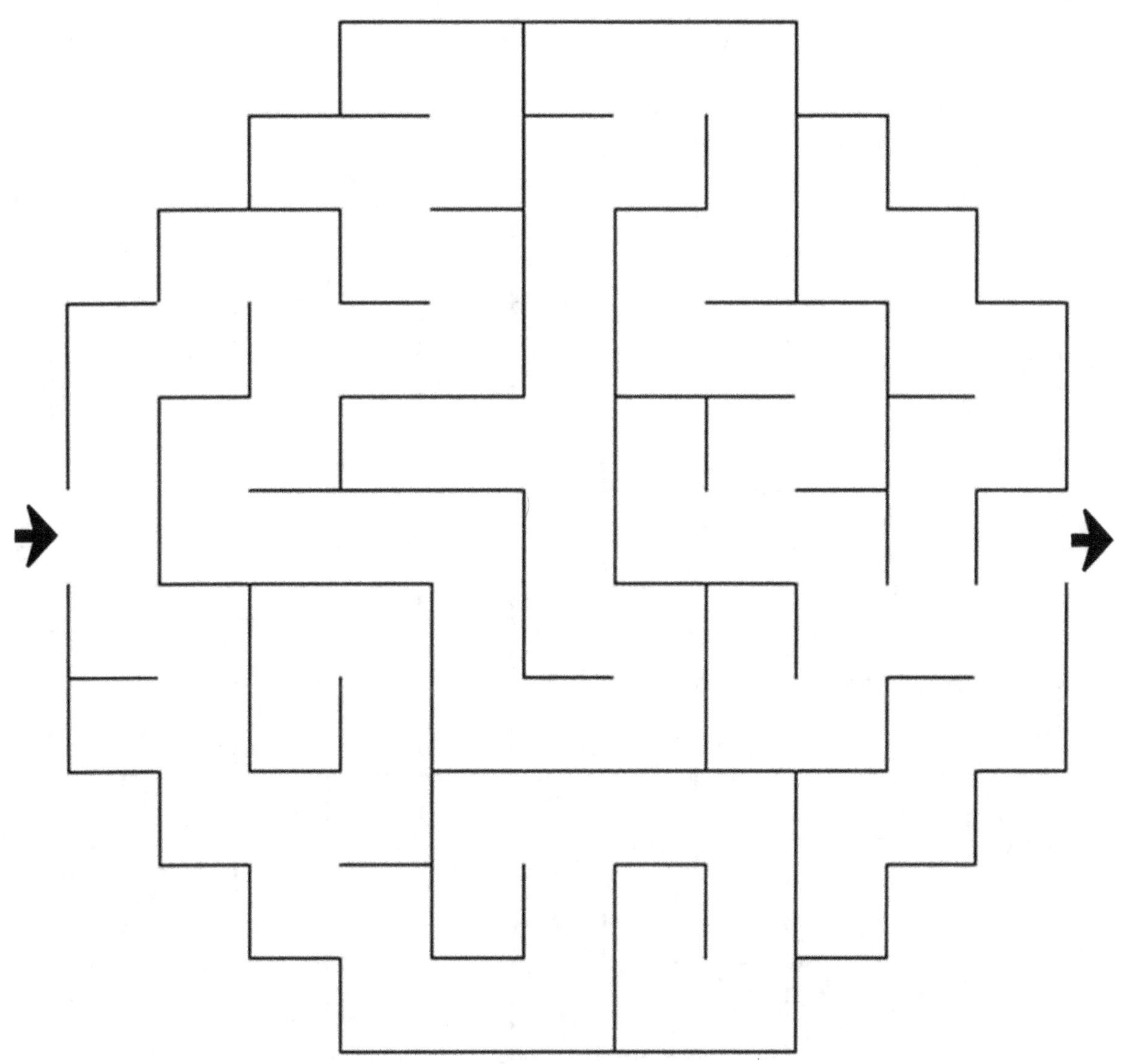

Name: ______________________   Date: ____________

76. Super - Difficult

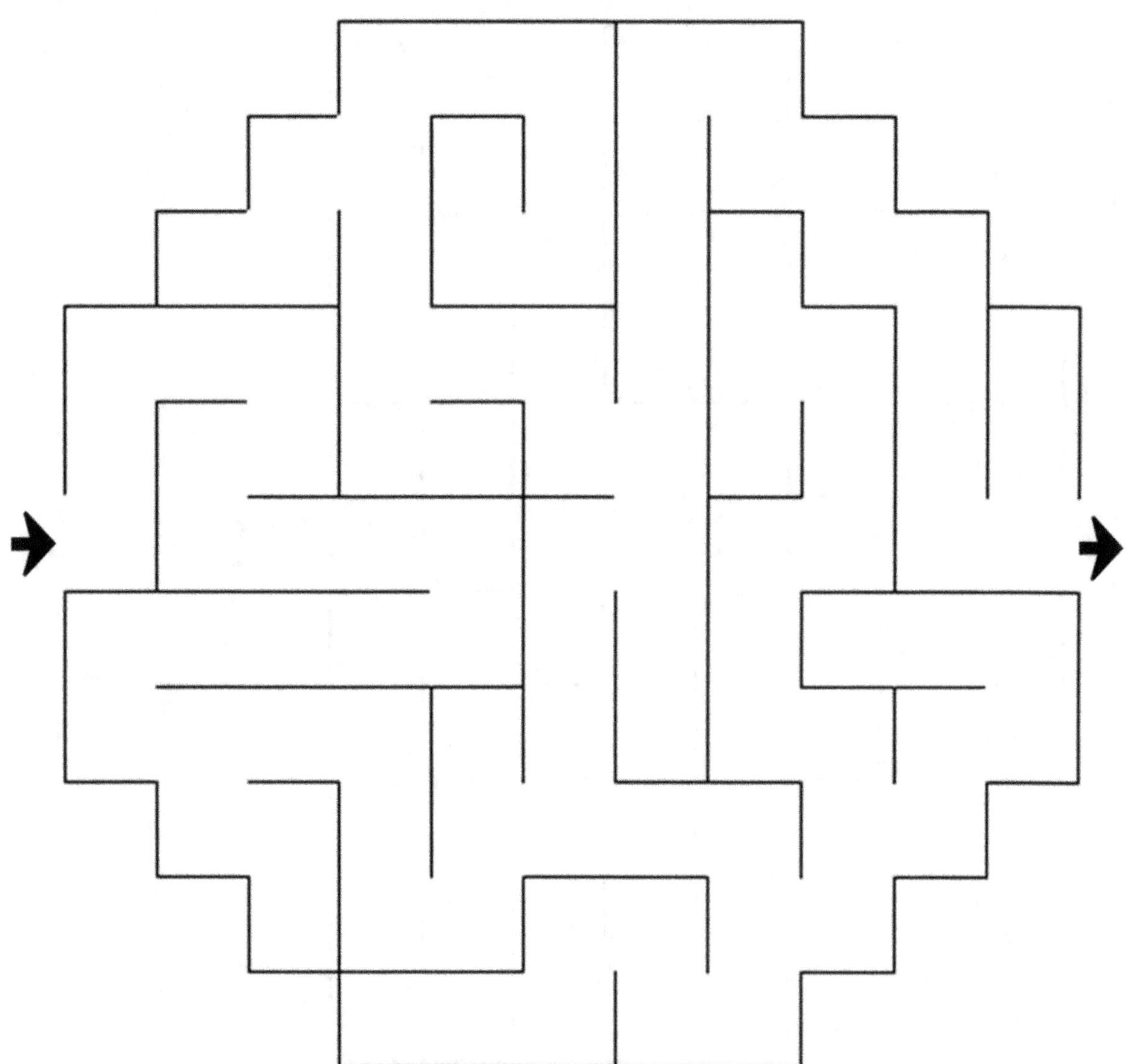

Kindergarten Mazes

Name: _______________________   Date: _____________

77. Super - Difficult

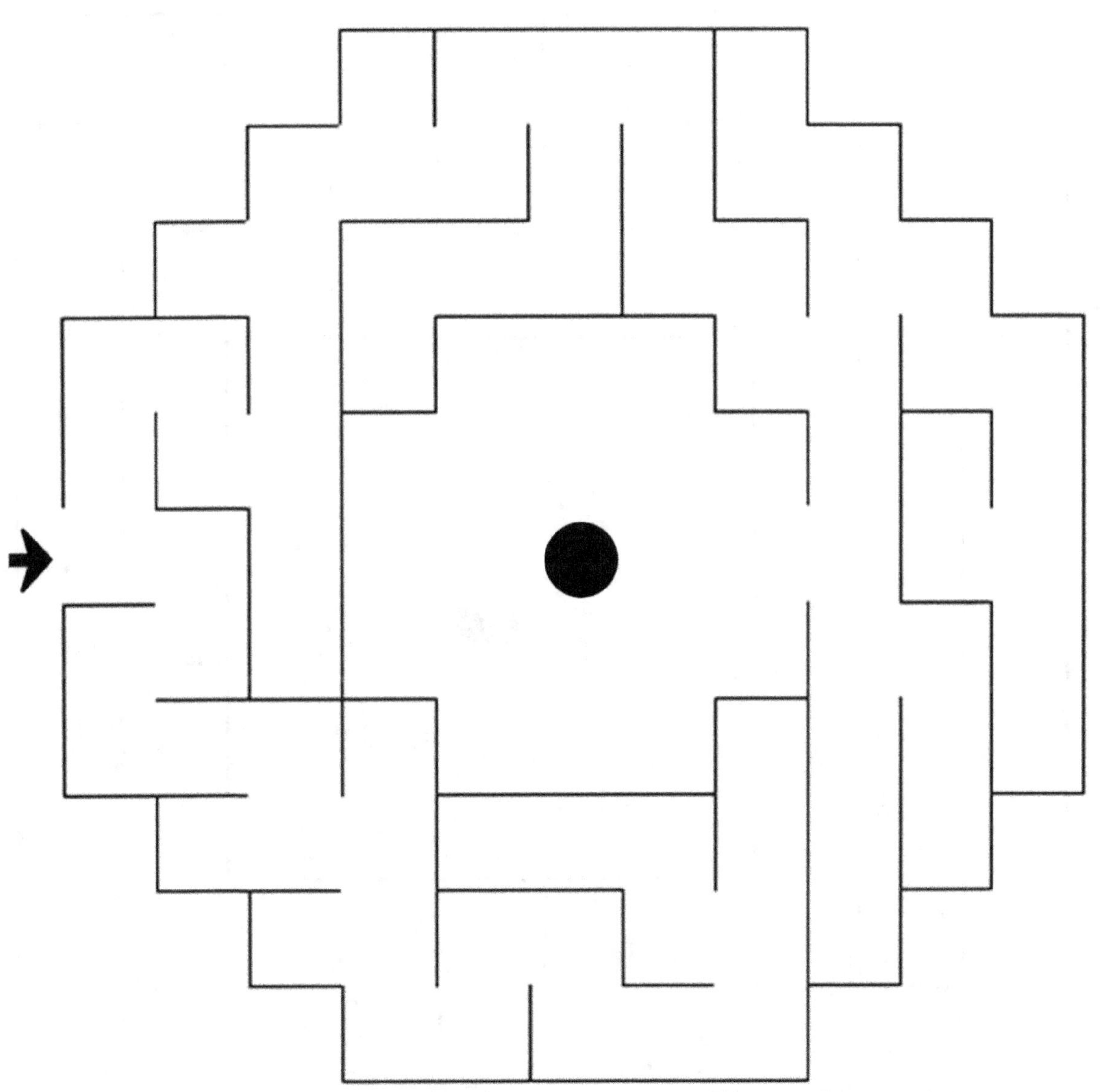

Name: _____________________   Date: _____________

78. Super - Difficult

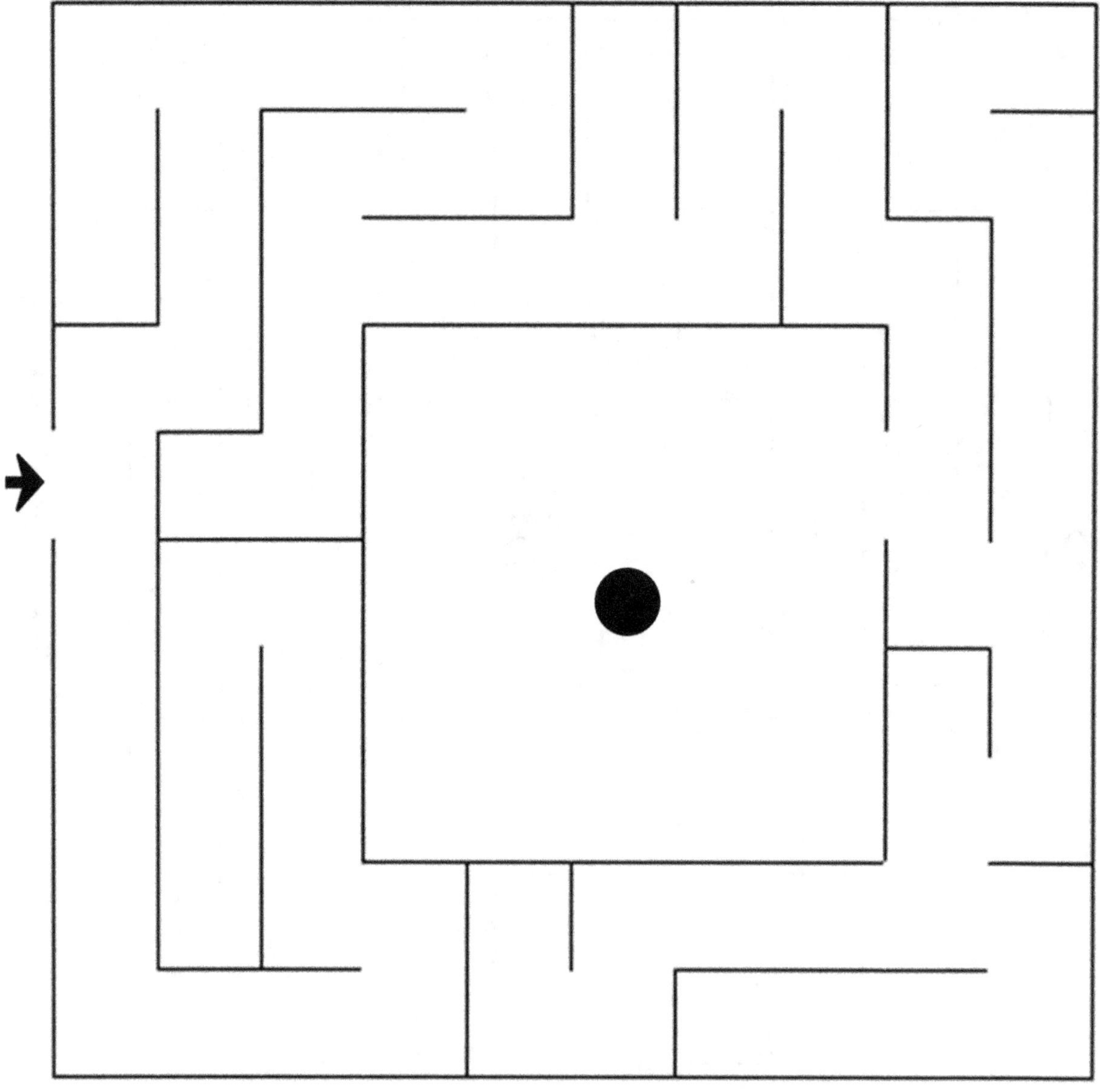

Also Available by the Same Authors:

Kindergarten Sudoku
4x4 Sudoku Puzzles for Kids

More Kindergarten Sudoku
4x4 Classic Sudoku Puzzles for Kids

The Big Book of Kindergarten Sudoku
4x4 Sudoku Puzzles for Kids

Beyond Kindergarten Sudoku
6x6 Sudoku Puzzles for Kids

Kindergarten Puzzles – Level 1
Simple Puzzles, Worksheets, and Activities for Kids

Kindergarten Puzzles – Level 2
Simple Puzzles, Worksheets, and Activities for Kids